LONDON TRANSPORT

BUSES & COACHES

1947

LONDON TRANSPORT

BUSES & COACHES

1947

Includes 1948 supplement

John A.S. Hambley

Published in 1997 by
Harold Martin & Redman Ltd

in conjunction with JOHN A.S. HAMBLEY
7 Linden Road,
Dunstable,
Beds. LU5 4NZ

Additional text and research by David A. Ruddom

British Library Cataloguing in Publication Data
A catalogue record for this book is available from the British Library

ISBN 1 901394 05 0

Designed and produced by Harold Martin & Redman Ltd.
Printed and bound in Great Britain.

C41 is parked at the Amersham garage complex with part of the earlier building being occupied by the War Agriculture Committee, one of the many Government Agencies set up during the 1939-45 conflict. A view of this vehicle after its sale by London Transport appears in the 1955 volume of this series of books.

Acknowledgements

Much of the photographic material contained within this book has been loaned from the collections of enthusiasts and historians and all concerned are warmly thanked for their personal enthusiasm and the encouragement they have given to me. They include: G.F.Baddeley, Bob Burrell, C.Carter, Alan B.Cross, the Docklands Museum, John Gascoine, J.C.Gillham, Peter Gomm, W.J.Haynes, Laurie Housden, D.W.K.Jones, S.E.Letts, John Lines, the London Trolleybus Preservation Society, K.A.V.Newley, the Omnibus Society, Norman Rayfield, Michael Rooum, David A.Ruddom, R.H.G.Simpson, John Smith of Lens of Sutton, John G.S.Smith, Sheila Taylor of the London Transport Museum, Whitbread Archive and Frank Willis. As with all previous volumes which have been published and now cover the scene unbroken from 1939 to 1956, many photographs have been used from the author's own extensive collection and some bear no indication of origin. As ever I am always pleased to acknowledge in later volumes any photographer or copyright owner who subsequently identifies his or her ownership.

The ever growing number of publications produced by the various organisations specialising in the study of the road transport history of London have again been consulted for factual information. The PSV Circle sereis of class histories, London area News Sheets and the summaries issued for earlier years have been used for vehicle information. For route information reference has been made to the publications of LOTS and the Omnibus Society. Many individuals have added their own personal contributions and to everyone involved thanks are extended for your continued help.

As usual my wife Iris and David Ruddom's wife Enid have shown great patience and forbearance in our quest which has involved long hours to bring this book to fruition.

Publisher's Note

If you have a collection of prints, some of which you feel might be appropriate for this series of books and which you would be prepared to lend, then please get in touch with me at the address shown earlier in this book. Equally if you have an interesting or unusual negative, arrangements can be made for this to be printed by Kevin Lane who, as well as providing a service for developing and printing black and white postcard prints, is the author of a number of transport books which have been commissioned and published by Ian Allan Ltd. Prints are also purchased if suitable for inclusion and any material from 1933 onwards would be considered.

A printed listing of all the vehicles shown in this series of books is available in fleet number order. The list gives fleet number, registration number, route or service engaged on, location, source of photograph and year and page number of the book in which it is published. A listing in route number order is also available but only covers the books for 1939 - 46 and 1948 - 1956. It is hoped to include the 1947 book in a later edition of the route number listing but this is not possible at the moment. These listings are only available direct from the author at Dunstable and are priced at £5.00 each. Please state whether you require fleet number or route number order when ordering.

Introduction

The transition from the war years to peacetime conditions slowly ground on during the year of 1947 although operating conditions for London Transport continued to deteriorate. During the year the five day week was generally introduced in the manufacturing sector of industry while further government wartime innovations were amended to add to the gradual return to peacetime activities.

The year got under way with a small number of service improvements made possible by the recent entry into service of the last of the Leyland STD class vehicles and the continuing delivery of the new TD class of single deck bus all of which were sent to Muswell Hill. The atrocious weather conditions experienced from late January through to mid March only exacerbated the difficulties however. The programme of renovation to the backlog of vehicles requiring attention expanded with the despatch of a number of buses to outside contractors which brought some relief to the overstretched Chiswick Works.

Although the number of new vehicles owned at the year end had increased it must be remembered that a number of the older types were in an unserviceable condition. The deficiencies in roadworthy vehicles, particularly at peak times, were eventually to prove too great and in October the Passenger Vehicle Operators' Association were approached resulting, after negotiation, of something in the order of 350 coaches of very diverse origins being hired by the LPTB together with drivers. Conductors and fuel were supplied by the Board.

The major historical occurrence of the year with regard to the bus fleet must be the first deliveries of the post-war RT class. This significant milestone was reached in April when RT402 mounted with Weymann bodywork arrived at Chiswick on the 28th. From this date onwards Londoners could look forward to a gradual process over the next few years of the renewal of the fleet with comfortable and reliable vehicles. Four garages - Leyton, Croydon, Potters Bar and Bromley - were proudly operating these buses by the end of the year.

As the year came to a close another event occurred in London bus history of some significance with the end of the London Passenger Transport Board and the new London Transport Executive taking over from the 1st of January 1948.

As regards details of the fleet, 108 of the well worn LT class together with 72 STs were earmarked for scrapping or scrapped during the year with many serviceable parts being returned to keep other members of the classes on the road. 43 STLs were withdrawn from service, many finding further uses on learner duties or their chassis put to one side to be finally fitted with service vehicle bodies. 2 T class vehicles, numbers 19 and 29, were dismantled by the Board. New vehicles into stock and service numbered 157 RTs and the last 21 of the first order for single deck TDs.

Route alterations continued to be mainly cosmetic during the early part of the year, many relating to adjustments for peak hour requirements. New routes introduced during the year were 146, 150, 153, 240A, 305A, 351 and 486. The biggest programme of route changes was introduced on 12th November which is perhaps indicative of the beginnings of improvement with the assistance of the hired coaches and the arrival of the post-war RTs. Most notable in those changes were the exchange of north London terminals between the 59/159 group of routes and the 53A and in the Country Area the split of the long 321 service into two routes.

An interesting series of special late night bus services for the benefit of MPs and staff of the House of Commons when late sitting occurred was started in March, which added to the Board's commitments but in the event were little used and soon withdrawn. At the end of the year some of the open staircase LTs made surplus by the new RTs were used to provide replacement bus services while the new Central Line extensions to Newbury Park and Woodford were completed.

Only a few weeks before being demoted to learner duties STL76 operates from Bromley, the same garage from which it had first entered service in January 1933. The 138 route was renumbered from 232 on 27th November 1940 when double deck operation with STLs replaced the former T class vehicles. In July of the year under review the bus last operated in passenger service and spent the last eighteen months of its life as a training vehicle at a variety of garages until it was scrapped exactly sixteen years after first taking to the road. (Omnibus Society)

The ten year old LPTB bodied TF1 is loaned back to its original owners in this November view taken in Lancaster Place while the vehicle is helping out on Route 1 between Lewisham and Marylebone. A fresh coat of paint has been applied since its appearance in the 1946 book of this series and when compared with the picture in the 1952 book it is apparent that this colour scheme proved to be short lived. The trafficator arm has not fully retracted which was common with vehicles fitted with these devices. The horse drawn delivery dray, still permitted in busy Central London, and an RAF vehicle numbered RAF125787 are typical of the 1947 scene. The usual weekday allocation to this route would have been an ST from Catford or Cricklewood garages. (G.F.Ashwell)

Delivered in June 1945 with an all brown paint finish, Massey bodied G183 would have to wait until March 1948 before receiving the more conventional Central Area bus livery. The Royal Forest Hotel at Chingford is the familiar background for this Barking garaged bus on Route 145 which carries duty plate 97. At the time most Central Area garages worked with separate sequences for each route but BK and their near neighbours U, both of whom had many interworked schedules, each operated one sequence and so such a high duty number was fairly unique to the eastern part of London. (S.L.Poole)

Oxted Station buildings in wood cladding with a 'Southern' inscribed timetable panel and a semaphore signal beside a gas lantern surely evoke a bygone era. When you add Leyland Cub C24 in use on Route 464 and seen here making its way to Holland, the picture is complete reminding one of the simple ways of travel before the mass arrival of the motor car. After its service with London Transport, this bus departed for the warm areas worked by the South Western Omnibus Co.(Ceylon) Ltd. (D.A.Ruddom collection)

LT52, the lead vehicle of this trio standing outside Upton Park garage, carries a blind for a rail replacement bus service. The extension of the Central Line from Leytonstone to Woodford and Newbury Park necessitated the withdrawal of the LNER train service from Liverpool Street to the Woodford loop via Ilford and Roding Valley after the 29th November. Nineteen open staircase LTs provided a replacement bus service but this was reduced to fifteen in the middle of December when the Central Line extension was commissioned and the Ilford to Newbury Park section of the bus service withdrawn. (D.W.K.Jones)

This and another picture in this book seem to suggest the crew changes at Godstone garage were rather lethargic and time consuming operations. STL2671, waiting patiently while working the 411 from Croydon to Reigate via Caterham and Godstone, first entered service in June 1942 operating around Amersham and district. Later in that year it was moved to the southern area of operations to replace ST class vehicles on Routes 409 and 411 in similar hilly terrain to that it had experienced in Buckinghamshire. The body in this instance is of the STL17/1 variety, recognisable by the lack of a route number blind box and non-opening windows at the front of the upper deck. Note also the unmatched front mudguards, the chassis being delivered from AEC with their standard nearside fitment while the offside example is part of the LPTB built body. (M.Rooum)

Park Royal bodied G198 was photographed at the Green Man, Leytonstone terminus in use on Route 66 on 12th April. The quick return to peacetime activities by Butlin's Holiday Camps has already been mentioned in this series of books and the front advertisements provide another example. Although not immediately noticeable in a black and white photograph, the bus is in a livery of brown and yellow ochre with a pinkish brown roof, not receiving the familiar London livery until March 1949. (V.C.Jones)

RT15, like the great majority of the 2RT2 vehicles, kept its original body, number 280, throughout its existence with London Transport. The numbers 280 to 429 were the body numbers used for RT2 to RT151 and they were allocated to each vehicle as and when they were completed in the time honoured fashion that was the practice at Chiswick Works. Thus RT15 was the first vehicle completed in December 1939 being one of seven to enter service on 2nd January 1940 from Chelverton Road on Route 37. After a relatively uneventful career it was sold to F.Ridler of Twickenham in April 1963. (R.H.G.Simpson)

This fine rear end view of LT95 well illustrates the last outside staircase buses delivered new to the LGOC. This batch of LTs seemed to have great endurance and you could still board such an antiquated machine right through to 1949 when the last were removed from public service. The date on which this photograph was taken outside the Piccadilly Hotel is 28th June. (A.B.Cross)

C7, with a good load, waits while passengers sort themselves out on its journey to Warlingham by way of Route 453. The public footpath signposted to Oakley Road and the Sunnyside Estate situated at Upper Warlingham confirm that in a short while the bus will arrive at its destination, probably with a sigh of relief. In later years this route would become RT operated and the extra capacity was sorely needed if this view is anything to go by. (D.A.Ruddom collection)

ST770 carries running plates ON6 for its use on Route 79 and is seen arriving at Alperton. The operating garage opened on 7th June 1939 with a complement of 57 STLs. This ST moved in on 3rd January 1946 staying until 2nd September 1949 when it transferred to Upton Park. It only remained there for six days, leaving on the 8th for the scrapping fields of Daniels. I don't think Wisk survives on the supermarket shelves of today but 'Woman's Own' can still be found. (A.B.Cross)

Ransomes, Sims and Jefferies bodied ST1105 was once operated by the East Surrey Traction Co.Ltd. carrying their fleet number 237 while being technically on loan from the LGOC. Of interest are its Surrey PG registration and the squared off driver's cab. The batch were initially delivered in 1930 for use on the 406 route which operated between Kingston and Redhill but after the formation of the LPTB they became scattered all through the Country Area system and this example operates from Reigate garage on Route 439, Reigate to Dorking and Holmwood. In later years some members even reached the Central Area before they had all been withdrawn from service, the last in February 1950. (J.G.S.Smith collection)

T244 has been pictured in this series of books before when in use in the Central Area but it is now seen in its more customary habitat. It was transferred to Luton garage in May 1946 and was to be a common sight in and around the town until August 1949 when it moved on to Willesden garage for its extended life as a relief vehicle. It was shunted around several garages before withdrawal in May 1950. Standing in Park Street with a background long since lost, it will soon be departing on a short working to Breachwood Green through the countryside lying to the east of Luton, much of which is now absorbed by Luton Airport. (P.Gomm collection)

When Route 67 commenced after the First World War in 1919 it ran from Stamford Hill to Raynes Park and subsequently to Earlsfield and Wimbledon. The Second World War saw it reduced to Stoke Newington to Waterloo and it remained a 'Cinderella' operation becoming the last route scheduled for ST operation in 1950. It finally succumbed in the first round of Central Area bus cuts on 20th August 1958 following the prolonged strike in that year. Its unique section down Chancery Lane then passed to 171. ST740 operating from Tottenham garage is seen in Sandell Street, Waterloo by the Union Jack Club, having just departed on its journey to Stoke Newington (J.G.S.Smith collection)

ST1107 stands in the Watford High Street garage driveway having worked in from Route 334A. This was the variant of 334 which ran from Watford Junction to Watford (Met) Station with peak hour extensions to Watford-by-Pass (Brockley Rise), a destination more familiar to most readers of this book as Aldenham Works. Within Watford it ran between the Junction and High Street via Queens Road, a journey which nowadays would involve crashing through the Harlequin Shopping Centre. (S.L.Poole)

This unique bus, easily identifiable as ST530 by its rebuilt upper deck, has been featured in earlier editions of this series of books but was thought worthy of inclusion once again. In use on Route 39 from Chalk Farm garage it is seen at Southfields Station where Battersea garage's STL1624 follows on the same route. (D.A.Ruddom collection)

In use within the City of Southampton for what could best be described as an extended loan, ST885, with driver about to shut the primitive cab door, is seen outside the impressive Hants & Dorset Omnibus Co. building. This ex-Tilling ST together with ST845 were the last of the wartime loans to be returned to London Transport in February 1948 having first gone to Hants & Dorset in May 1944. Interestingly both buses had already been on loan with other operators prior to this, having left London in December 1941 and only briefly returning before being sent into exile again. On its return to London ST885 was used as a training vehicle, being one of those whose seating was reduced to just four double seats for this role,. It was scrapped in the spring of 1949 having originally entered service in August 1930. (G.F.Baddeley)

The first nine AEC Regent chassis built in 1929 were fitted with open stair case bodies by Short Brothers of Rochester to the chassis manufacturer's specification. National of London took four of them while two went on demonstration tours, one of which was exported to South America. The remaining three vehicles were used by three interested operators in the British Isles. Chassis number 661008 was loaned to the LGOC with its 51 seat body and registered UU6610 being handed over to the subsidiary East Surrey Traction Company entering service on Route 414 between Redhill and Horsham. It later went to Autocar Ltd. before returning to Chiswick eventually to be purchased and still later allocated its fleet number ST1139, having been numbered 255 by East Surrey. A common sight in the Windsor area after its wartime sojourn in Coventry it was eventually withdrawn from service in September 1948 being scrapped the following month. (J.Gascoine collection)

Two of the original Gardner powered 'Bluebird' LTs never received AEC engine replacements from withdrawn vehicles. The two were LT1420 and LT1423 and unfortunately due to being powered by non-standard units both were withdrawn from service before the end of 1948 while the others soldiered on into the following year. LT1420 with ST390 and two TFs are seen parked in Grays resting from their task of helping keep the Country Department on the move. Originally when eight of these 60 seater giants were transferred into Grays in April they could be seen operating on Routes 370 and 371A but after a short period they were restricted to the latter probably due to their length. (L.Housden collection)

T277b had a chequered career, having first entered service from Tunbridge Wells garage and put to use on the Green Line service from Royal Tunbridge Wells to Oxford Circus. Gradually with the delivery of the newer 10T10 coaches during 1938 and 1939, these 1930/1 built coaches were either disposed of, rebodied, converted to service vehicles or, with little alteration, put to use on Country Area bus services. With the outbreak of the war this particular vehicle was converted to a staff ambulance being identified as 434W and it was not until September 1945 that reconversion to passenger use as now viewed took place. Here it is seen at Uxbridge working from Windsor on Route 458 but eventually it moved into the Central Area to work from Hounslow, Bromley and Kingston before being disposed of in May 1950. In later years it was to be used as a caravan and can be seen in this role in the supplement to the 1946 book of this series. (J.G.S.Smith collection)

TD29, having just arrived from Weymanns Ltd. of Addlestone, is viewed standing within the Chiswick Works complex prior to entry into passenger service from Muswell Hill garage. Composite construction was used for the construction of the body with seating for 33 passengers and being built for Central Area use there was no need for a door to the passenger saloon. The customary bonnet plate for LT fleet number was not fitted to these vehicles, transfers being applied directly to the bonnet side in similar fashion to other early post-war deliveries. Note also the chrome radiator surround with offset filler cap. (L.T.Museum H/16784)

Upon their return to normal duties after the war the 9T9s continued with the bus work to which they had been relegated when the 10T10 coaches arrived in 1938. They were scattered throughout the Country Area with a small number contained within the Central Area. Very occasionally some members of the batch (T403 - T452) strayed on to Green Line work as we shall see later in this book. It was an advantage therefore that they still carried their route board brackets. T444 has attracted a good load before departing from the St.Mary's Square terminus at Hitchin on a journey through the villages of Hertfordshire to St.Albans, its home town. (M.Rooum)

With the influx of new RTs at Leyton garage the open staircase type of LT was made redundant from its long standing usual haunts. LT68 found a new home at Sidcup garage and it is seen in use on Route 21 heading for Well Hall Station. Later demoted to learner duties it finally succumbed to the breaker's torches in 1949 at the ripe old age of nineteen. Blast damaged windows still have to be attended to in the shop immediately beside the bus and the pyramids of tinned food reminds one of the days before refrigerator ownership was common and freezers were a thing of the future. (A.B.Cross)

Against a shabby and indistinct public house sign equally shabby LT1057 heads for Hounslow on the 237 route from Chertsey. The bus however would be transformed by Marshalls of Cambridge between May and September 1949, reappearing almost like a new vehicle. Unfortunately for Hounslow garage staff they would not have the pleasure of this LT after its rebuild as it then returned to service from Muswell Hill. (A.B.Cross)

When delivered to Chiswick on 5th February 1944, this Park Royal bodied Guy Arab II with fleet number G125 was finished in an all over grey livery due to the shortage of paint and had wooden slatted seating. Red and off white paint was applied in November 1944 but the uncomfortable wooden seats remained until October 1947. In the main London Guys were inflicted on suburban dwellers but Route 23 from Marylebone to Becontree Heath introduced these delights to Oxford Street, Holborn and the City. This bus remained at Barking garage for the whole of its working life in London which ended in January 1952 with eventual shipment to Ceylon. Here it waits at the Marylebone terminus. (W.J.Haynes)

The food situation in the period immediately after the war is well highlighted here by the side advertisement carried on this ex-Tilling STL which reads 'Join the crusade against bread waste; we must not waste while others want'. A discreet note adds that the space had been kindly presented by Hovis Ltd. (presumably to the Ministry of Food). Unfortunately the identification of the bus remains a mystery due to the custom of carrying the rear number plate at the top of the lower saloon bulkhead inside the platform area. It is however one of those registered AGF821-840 being garaged at Bromley and is seen at Bromley North soon to depart for Hayes, Coney Hall on Route 138. (L.Housden collection)

Standing within the Chiswick complex on 5th October, Park Royal bodied G129 awaits the removal of the wooden slatted seating with which it first entered service in March 1944 ready for replacement with the more comfortable moquette type. The all over grey paint scheme first applied due to the shortage of red or brown paint had been replaced on a previous visit to the works in December 1944. A resident of Barking garage, it would ply the BK services until December 1950 when it would be transferred to Seven Kings as a training vehicle. Final withdrawal came in February 1952 and eventual disposal to W.North & Sons followed in December of the same year. (J.C.Gillham)

At Camberwell Green on its journey to South Croydon by way of the 68 route, Norwood's STL484 passes the trailing crossover of the tram tracks just south of Walworth Depot. The trees and the open windows give the impression of a warm spring day. The bus was eventually to receive one more overhaul in October 1950 retaining the body, number 14223, it currently carries and was then to continue in passenger service until withdrawn in February 1953. (J.G.S.Smith collection)

Camberwell garaged STL578 is viewed at the Kings Oak, High Beach deserted by its crew, which just might have included the photographer, and is set for its return journey to Clapham Common on Route 35A. When first entering service in October 1934 this bus was coded 7STL3/2 and was fitted with a secondhand petrol engine and pre-selector gearbox. From its April 1939 overhaul and body change it was classified as a 2/16STL18 indicating a modified body to suit the diesel engine then fitted. So the vehicle remained until its withdrawal in October 1953. Exported through the docks of Ostend via Dover the bus probably saw out its life in much the same condition. (W.J.Haynes)

STL2107 received one of the new STL19 lowbridge bodies from the batch of twenty built by LPTB in 1942/43 which were mounted on to chassis then passing through Chiswick Works. These bodies represented the only low height type ever built by the LPTB but the STL family connection is clearly visible. The only non-standard fitment was the hopper type ventilator to the front bulkhead window on the lower deck, still fitted in this view but removed subsequently. The bus was photographed at Rayners Lane before departure for Northwick Park Station by way of the familiar Harrow Weald Route 230. (K.A.V.Newley collection)

T7 waits to take up duties on Route 216 on a short working to the 'Flower Pot' at Sunbury while the T behind will work right through to Staines. Prior to January 1941 the route was one man operated using the new little 20 seat CRs which had entered service at Kingston at the time war was declared. After this date a mixture of the two types could be seen in service on the route until single deck LTs became the main allocation from September 1942. In this view taken sometime in August, the passengers are clearly seen seated in the longitudinal seating facing inwards which had graced this front entrance bus since 1942, an arrangement it was to keep until disposal which took place in August 1949. (V.C.Jones)

This rear view of RT181 at the Woodford Bridge terminus shows the clean cut profile at the rear of these vehicles. At the time our eyes expected to see a roof box on the rear of an RT but in time the bare dome became accepted. Note the white painted disc on the bottom lower panel, a practice introduced during the wartime blackout which was only discontinued with deliveries of new buses from May 1948 onwards, some three years after the ending of hostilities.

This first day in service view of RT402 at Victoria on 10th May gives a good impression of the startling way in which the bus stood out from contemporary vehicles. Leyton garage was the first to receive the new order of post-war RTs but before the year end Croydon, Potters Bar and Bromley also had them in operation. Standing beside the new bus G66, also bodied by Weymann, operates from Tottenham garage on Route 76 which had been associated with the type since their introduction in 1942 but it is passed by as all eyes are on the brand new vehicle. (S.A.Newman)

Pressed into use on stage carriage service LTC21 must have been a most unsuitable candidate for such work. Having a narrow saloon gangway, high backed bulky seating and no stanchions or supports of any sort, the conductor must have found life difficult. The precarious position in which London Transport found itself however meant that any roadworthy bus or coach could be found in most unusual situations. Post war deliveries of new vehicles and hired vehicles gradually eased the conditions in the coming years. In this view taken in Meadfield Street, Roehampton a more usual 2RT2 engaged on the same route is parked in front of the Weymann bodied, petrol engined six wheeled coach while behind a mid-1930s Ford Popular Series Y faces oncoming traffic. (L.Housden collection)

LT449 with the familiar background of the Green Man, Leytonstone terminus awaits departure to Dagenham Dock on Route 139 which had been introduced as a new weekday peak hour service on 21st January 1942 to cater primarily for workers at Dagenham and to replace a rather rambling extension of Route 41. Originally entering service in June 1931 the bus had carried a Park Royal built body, number 11616, from a batch of ninety numbered 11545 to 11634. At the end of its service in London during January 1949 it carried this Strachan manufactured example numbered 11713, the second to last received from this organisation. (W.J.Haynes)

Hatfield based front entrance STL995b clearly shows the use of the suffix letter B to denote a vehicle of bus standard. This vehicle was eventually withdrawn from service in March 1949 and its poor condition is evident already in this view dated 27th November. The STL6 bodywork is of unmistakably handsome LPTB manufacture. Sidelights were originally located in the between deck cantrail but more standard units have now been fitted. A route number stencil holder has been added to the entrance window in addition to the larger plate holder above with the intention of enabling rear illumination from the saloon lights. Between the two is the inscription 'To seat 52 passengers, 23 lower, 29 upper' which was an increase from the original 19/29 configuration made possible by the fitting of a longitudinal double seat over the wheel arches in place of the luggage stands in October 1939. (L.T.Museum U41619)

Upton Park's ST216 heads through the Becontree estate for Ford Works at Dagenham, which was a bifurcation from the main route through to Blackwall Tunnel which turned westward at 'The Chequers'. G, ST, LT and STL class vehicles were the mainstay of the service until RTLs made their debut in 1952. Only twenty ex-LGOC STs received registration numbers in the GJ series, their numbers allocated when the completed vehicle was ready for the licensing shop at Chiswick.

Behind the Queen Victoria at North Cheam two distinctly different types of bus wait for departure on Route 151 to Carshalton, Culvers Avenue. Interestingly official timetables referred to this as Hackbridge, Reynolds Close but the blind compilers thought otherwise at the time. I know which bus I would have travelled on in all probability at the time: I would have chosen D273 being such a gleaming new addition to the fleet but with hindsight a chance to still ride on an ex-Tilling ST should not have been missed. ST996, now seventeen years of age, was withdrawn in January of the following year, Sutton garage being its final operating base. (A.B.Cross)

The LTC class of coach were occasionally used on Green Line work. Here, parked at the Minories Bus & Coach Station at Aldgate, LTC17 has its blinds set for a journey on Route 720 as far as its home base rather than the full route which would have taken it to Bishops Stortford. A nearside view of this coach is shown in the 1948 book of this series, again on the same route in the same location, but careful inspection of the two reveals that in the later print the headlights and spotlight have been repositioned.

1947 marked the entry into service of the post-war RT. The first Park Royal bodied example, RT152, began passenger duties on 23rd May from Leyton garage on Route 10 as part of the programme for the replacement of ageing open staircase LTs. It is seen here at Victoria Station being admired by a driver whose look gives the impression that he would like to be in charge of such a thing of beauty. The first RT to enter service had been Weymann bodied RT402, almost a full fortnight earlier. The large oblong nearside mirror fitted to the deeply valanced canopy and the panel frame for notices above the rear wheel arch are worthy of note. Only the first few vehicles from both body manufacturers incorporated the frame, a change of policy dictating that notices were now to be affixed to lower saloon windows. (S.A.Newman)

The stone setts in the Market Place at Romford on which the stalls were placed on market days are still there today but no longer does it double as the main London to Brentwood and Chelmsford road. LT1389 pauses on its journey to Chadwell Heath on the Sunday only allocation provided by Seven Kings garage which was to become a daily responsibility on 12th November. The bus was to be scrapped in the opening months of 1949. The ill matching headlights, while by no means unique among the pre-war vehicles operated by London Transport are very evident in this picture. (J.G.S.Smith collection)

The 9T9 sub class of vehicle occasionally strayed back on to Green Line work after the war, these having been demoted to bus work upon their return from other uses during the period of hostilities. Sometime during December, on one of those bright but crisp days, T409 substitutes for another coach on Route 711. This High Wycombe coach, pulling away from the stop at Clapham Common, is still a relative stranger to South London, the route only having been extended beyond central London to High Wycombe in place of 724 on 12th November. (V.C.Jones)

Although Upton Park is not a garage associated at this time with STLs it appears from the fleet number on the roof that STL2068 was once garaged there but has moved on since and now operates from Holloway garage. Here it is working one of that shed's duties on Route 134 from Victoria Station to Hadley Highstone. The remains of the white disc on the lower panelling are still discernible. This is one of the few original batch of Park Royal bodied STL15 class which still retains an all metal Park Royal body. The bus was withdrawn from service in August 1949, its chassis reappearing as the basis for SRT134 in January 1950 while the body was scrapped. (A.B.Cross)

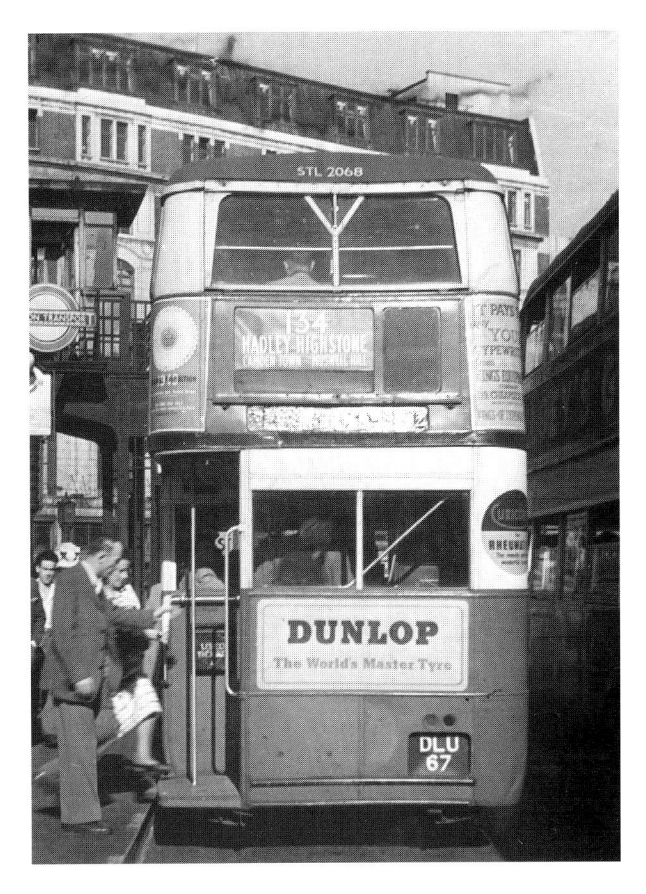

Standing at the 'Green Man', Leytonstone terminus of Route 10A on 12th April, STD154 is seen in company with a bus nearly nineteen years its elder in the shape of LT941 parked closely behind. Purchased as a stop gap measure prior to the arrival of the RT class, these STDs were basically a standard Leyland Titan PD1 chassis with Leyland 56 seat highbridge bodywork incorporating minor modifications to suit London Transport requirements. During their years with London Transport two overhauls were given to the class but no body changes ever took place. The body numbers of the batch were 1336 to 1400 and the first Park Royal built RT, 152, carried number 1401 continuing the series. (V.C.Jones)

Originally it was intended to build 102 vehicles similar to STL83 but upon the takeover of the LGOC by London Transport in July 1933, the final twenty two were cancelled. The allocated fleet numbers, STL131 - 152 were therefore never used and although the highest numbered reached STL2701, there were never more than 2679 STLs owned by LT. Departing from Bromley garage the STL carries a well adjusted route blind for its journey as TB3 to Well Hall Station at Eltham. In the years 1948/49 it migrated to the Country Area to be operated by Two Waters before returning to Bromley for a short while prior to its withdrawal from service in October 1949 (Vanguard Bus Prints)

Parked beside Victoria garage, Q14 takes a well earned rest while the occupants have vanished for some refreshments. An L plate is carried by this 4Q4 which has been diverted from its normal use as a bus in the Country Area. Its career had started in July 1935 at Dartford and lasted until it finished at Luton garage in February 1952. The revolutionary design of chassis embodied in these vehicles had the engine mounted, slightly inclined, on the offside of the chassis and was in production from 1933 to 1936, although two prototypes were completed in 1932 and deliveries were still being made after production ceased. Twenty three four wheel and one six wheel double deck and 319 single deck chassis were manufactured of which London Transport took 238 in total. (Lens of Sutton)

Hammersmith Broadway has always been a very busy road interchange with the confluence of a number of main traffic arteries. At twenty past one on Thursday 3rd July the scene is frozen for posterity. RT131 with advertising for Craven Plain cigarettes at 15 for 2/6d crosses on its short working 72 journey to Roehampton. An ST follows on Route 33 with its Picture Post eyes searching out the way to Hounslow while LT965 with John Bull advertising edges round to Hammersmith Bridge Road while making for Mortlake. Behind another Route 9 bus has its blind reset for Liverpool Street which probably indicates it will turn short in Hammersmith garage in Queen Caroline Street. A fair number of private cars vie for space in this busy scene. (L.T.Museum 19616)

Shortly after the western section of the long 321 route from Luton to Uxbridge was separated and renumbered 351 on 12th November ST1073 passes Rickmansworth Station en-route to Uxbridge. The steam locomotive carries the London Transport lining out on its tank and is a reminder that this was where in 1947 the change from electric to steam power occurred. Advertising of the period on the embankment includes a new housing development and a merchant who can supply timber, coal and coke for all uses. How times have changed in fifty years is dramatically summed up by this print. (A.B.Cross)

A busy Victoria Station forecourt with centre stage AEC Regal GN4417 which appears to have received recent attention judging by the newly silvered chassis parts underneath the body with its shiny mudguards. On loan to act as a relief this elderly vehicle of similar age to some LT class buses seen in the background, was owned by Sunbeam (C.J.Worsley) and seems to be attracting much attention and comment from the London Transport staff. It maybe that this was in October 1947 when hired coaches on LT routes were still a novelty hence the interest in this single decker as it waits for departure to Loughton Station on Route 38A. (A.B.Cross)

The 413 route described a horseshoe course from Chipstead to Brasted through the Kentish Weald around Sevenoaks and, as was customary for this type of route, used the type of blind display shown here rather than highlight the ultimate destination which might be reached in a more direct manner. Just why the road is closed behind T624 is not known but perhaps some reader can provide the answer. T624 was one of the 10T10s which remained in service with LPTB right through the war, much of it from Dunton Green garage as seen here. However on 12th November of the year under review the coach moved to Amersham and never again graced the lanes around Ide Hill and Brasted. (J.G.S.Smith collection)

RT425, which entered service in October from Leyton, is seen in wintry surroundings at the 'Horse and Well', Woodford Wells. The badly fitted slipboard on the bulkhead window reads 'Route 10A via Hollybush Hill & Highstone'. This dates the picture as taken in December when the 10A route was diverted via Southend Road, Maybank Road, George Lane and Hermon Hill due to work on the Central Line extension removing the level crossing in Eagle Lane before the bridge work at Snaresbrook was completed. An additional service between Woodford Wells and Leytonstone via Hollybush Hill was introduced to cover the normal route down Woodford High Road. Scheduled for LT operation it did see RTs from time to time as seen in this photograph. (S.L.Poole)

Utility D class vehicles were used to inaugurate the post-war Green Line routes 721 and 722 during March and April 1946 from Aldgate to Brentwood or Corbets Tey respectively. In August that year five STLs were transferred into Romford, London Road garage and given appropriate livery for working alongside the Ds. STL2523 was originally delivered in Central Area colours in June 1939 garaged at Hanwell. Both the Country and Central Areas received examples of these last pre-war STLs which featured wheel discs and Doverite covered sections of handrail. After less than two years a substantial number of the red variety were added to those already in green livery including this one in June 1941. The Chiswick built body, number 165, would stay matched with the chassis until in 1949 it was transferred to the chassis of STL2055, the original chassis being converted to become SRT56. Here at the busy Aldgate terminus it awaits departure on the 15 minute headway provided on Route 722 as far as Hornchurch. (J.Gascoine collection)

In 1932 the LGOC purchased twelve AEC Regal chassis to replace a similar number of Tilling Stevens petrol electric TS7 buses which had been employed on Route 109 since replacing single deck B type vehicles in 1925. Tilling built the bodies and operated the buses on behalf of the LGOC. All passed to the LPTB on 1st October 1933 and were given fleet numbers T307 to T318 still being used on the route which was renumbered 227 on 3rd October 1934. Waning in appearance some fifteen years on in its life, T318 as duty E9 rests at the Wake Arms in between operations on Route 242 which ran from there to Potters Bar Garage. Still with its petrol engine it was dismantled by the Executive in January 1949. (M.Rooum)

T391, a Dodson bodied coach originally owned by Bucks Expresses (Watford) Ltd., was renumbered from T307 in 1935 when the Country Area engineering records were transferred to Chiswick and it was found AEC Regals T307 to T318, then operated by Green Line Coaches, duplicated these numbers which were already carried by the 'Tilling' Ts, 307 - 318. Downgraded to a bus and fitted with a standard bus type front destination box it continued in its new role until June 1949 when it was sold to R.L.Daniels of Rainham for scrap. At sometime during the war years the passenger saloon door had been removed, while between August 1942 and April 1945 it performed its duties in grey livery. Here it is seen in Cromwell Road, Kingston in April in use on Route 218 on which it could be regularly found for many years. (K.A.V.Newley)

LTC14 with Holloway garage plate is pictured at Earls Court on Friday 16th May in use on the special shuttle between this venue and Olympia for the British Industries Fair. Interestingly this class of twenty four luxury touring coaches were built using petrol engines taken from LT class vehicles which were then being converted to diesel power. Initially they were housed at Old Kent Road (P) and the ex-Cambrian Landray garage at Brixton Hill (BT) which was closed on 1st January 1938. During 1949 and 1950 these vibration free coaches were re-engined using units from the array of double deckers then being scrapped in an exercise to rid the Executive of all petrol engined vehicles in this period. (F.Willis)

Route 10 had a variety of vehicles in use during the year and here STD106, one of the small batch of eleven Leyland Titan TD7 buses with Park Royal utility bodywork, crosses London Bridge on its way to Woodford Bridge pursued by an LT in service on Route 35. Delivered between December 1941 and August 1942 these buses were always garaged at Gillingham Street for their passenger revenue earning duties and they operated on most of GM's routes at one time or another. All were withdrawn from use in 1951 and put into store at Potters Bar garage, reappearing as staff buses and latterly as learners until they were finally disposed of between 1953 and 1955. (S.A.Newman)

D141 and D149 stand within the Minories Bus & Coach Station at Aldgate ready for their journeys to Brentwood on Route 721. In the background a further D class vehicle in company with a TF coach demonstrate the busy nature of this London Green Line terminal. While two of the Daimlers wear the earlier livery of green and white, D149 is finished with the newer two shades of green. An inspector is busy with the immediate proceedings as some potential passengers seem bewildered as to exactly which vehicle will be leaving first. (L.T.P.S.)

STD1 stands outside Golders Green Station sometime in November with a now redundant wartime shelter to the right of the picture with its customary flat reinforced concrete roof and substantial brickwork. The powerful sounding Leylands had provided Hendon garage's contribution to the 183 route since 28th May 1937. Six and a half years younger G97, operating from Alperton garage, waits for custom further out in the cobbled forecourt which in 1947 lacked any loading platforms or formal bay markings. (V.C.Jones)

Clay Hall garage was the initial recipient of STL1 to STL50 and put them into service during the early months of 1933 either on Route 8 and its derivatives operating between Old Ford and Willesden, Neasden or Kingsbury or on Route 160 between Old Ford and London Bridge replacing ST type vehicles in the process. Later in that year they began to be transferred to other garages being replaced by newer vehicles of the same class and their association with this north east London garage was brought to an abrupt end. By the early post-war period they were spread between five garages: PB, TB, TC, V and X and STL28 now housed at the latter operates on Route 7A at London Bridge. This route had been introduced in August 1946 and was extended from Acton Vale to Acton on 12th November of the year under review so this picture dates from the tail end of the year. (J.G.S.Smith collection)

The forty six buses which eventually became ST1085 to ST1088 and ST1091 to ST1132 with bodies built by Ransomes, Sims and Jeffries of Ipswich in the early months of 1930 were very similar to the body built by the LGOC for ST1. The first four were transferred from Autocar Services of Tunbridge Wells while the others had all be operated by the East Surrey Traction Company either having been owned by them or operated on behalf of the LGOC. The square cab and smaller route box aperture are similar to that fitted to ST1. ST1091 spent three years after the war in service at Hertford and is seen on 6th November ready for action on that garage's trunk route to Enfield. (L.T.Museum 22238)

An interesting view of various vehicles at Uxbridge Underground station is captured in this winter time picture with T302 as the main subject. From left to right, a 4Q4 with WT16 garage plates in use on Route 309 is slowly filling with passengers. The ex-Green Line coach, now bus T302, had been returned to peace time duties in July 1945 from its six year use as a staff ambulance and is working Route 458 which was a regular 7T7 operation from WR for many years. Over in the far background a roof box STL has attracted one passenger for its journey on Route 457 to Windsor, while all the missing crews are probably enjoying refreshments and congenial company within the staff canteen numbered 691J in the service vehicle fleet which can just be seen on the right. (A.B.Cross)

One could have the choice of riding on an STL or STD garaged at Victoria or a Merton D class vehicle or STL when travelling the 77A route during the period covered by this book. The three different types of bus representing three distinct periods in the history of London Transport, being pre-war, wartime or post-war delivered vehicles. Here on the Albert Embankment D88 had first entered service in June 1945 and was destined to reach the end of its operational career still being staffed by Merton personnel for use on all the garage's double decked routes except the 127 for which lowbridge vehicles were required. Some years later the bus moved on for further operation in Ceylon. (L.Housden collection)

A GW registration was more normally found on 'Bluebird' LTs but LT949, together with LT1232, shared the distinction of being the last of the LT5 variant of body to enter service in March 1932. This Mortlake garaged bus passes the Law Courts on its way to Liverpool Street on Route 9. Fitted from new with a diesel engine which came from one of the experimental ST oilers, the bus carried the code 4LT5/3. In March 1949 the body and chassis were separated being scrapped a few weeks apart. (R.Burrell)

Daily route 72 operated between Esher and East Acton using Chelverton Road, Putney garage RT type buses and this was supplemented but certainly not enhanced on Sundays by G class vehicles from Alperton garage for the expanded route Esher to North Wembley. Photographed at the Fountain public house in New Malden on 25th October, RT5 had received an overhaul a year previous at Chiswick Works, emerging carrying the body number 283 once fitted to RT20 and this accounts for the paint scheme now carried. Of interest is the fact that 30 of the original 150 production RT2 chassis finished their careers with London Transport carrying a different body to that with which they first entered service. (A.B.Cross)

Hammersmith garage had an on and off relationship over the years with Route 91, regaining an allocation on Saturdays on 27th November after an absence of three and a half years. One can almost hear the creaking of the sagging sixty seat body of LT1225 as it makes a left hand turn in the depths of its last winter in passenger service. In its first eighteen months of duty a petrol engine had powered this AEC Renown which it exchanged for a diesel unit in October 1933. It ended its days as an 11LT6/4, the same classification assigned to it in 1933 by the newly formed LPTB. (J.G.S.Smith collection)

APC55, a Bedford WLB of 1933 vintage with 20 seat Duple coachwork stands among an array of fine 30s built vehicles which have converged on Epsom Racecourse. This delightful vehicle was originally owned and operated by Sunshine Coaches Ltd. of Kingston Upon Thames and used in conjunction with two more elderly coaches on their stage service between the Surrey county town and Ashford via Hampton Court - a forerunner of the present day 216 route. The operator was absorbed by LPTB on 29th December 1933 and this vehicle became BD10. It was withdrawn from service in 1939 being disposed of to H.Lane, a dealer in south west London from whom it passed to two different owners at Loxwood before reaching its final home with E.J.Carter of Plummers Plain in the charming area lying between the North and South Downs in July 1947. (S.A.Newman)

The advertisement exhorts you to save for the future by buying National Savings Stamps and presumably aid the rebuilding of bomb sites such as that to the right of LT890 in Finsbury Square. Nowadays it seems strange that regulations required three axles for a vehicle with a length of 26feet, 9 and three eighth inches but that was the situation when this bus was built. The tidy condition of the vehicle is probably due to the renovation it had received at Mann Egerton's Norwich works during March and April 1946. (G.F.Ashwell)

ST1090 was one of two lowbridge bodied AEC Regents bought in 1930 by the Amersham and District Motor Bus & Haulage Co.Ltd. Oddly, whilst broadly similar, one was built by Strachan and the other (ST1089) by Short Bros. There were small differences between the two as examination of contemporary photographs will show. When the two vehicles first entered service they carried a maroon and cream livery but this was replaced in due course by the various styles of Country Area green. Eventually these two lowbridge vehicles joined very similar buses previously operated by the National Omnibus and Transport Company on behalf of the LGOC already operating Route 336 which originated back in 1921. (D.W.K.Jones)

Any old coach might be put to work on the Green Line network when the need arose although they may have been demoted to bus duties many years earlier. T270 was officially withdrawn from this type of work in March 1939 spending the interim months in store until converted to a staff ambulance in September. It was used in this capacity until October 1945 and was made ready for bus duties in April 1946, receiving suitable livery, fleet name and replacement of its two piece destination box with the single aperture seen here. It entered service from Windsor garage and on this occasion is about to set out as relief duty number WR110 on a journey up to London on Route 718.

Photographed at Windmill Road, Greenford, STD159 was one of nine of the class to be allocated to Hanwell garage when they were new during the last two months of 1946. They worked alongside STL type buses from HW and STs from Turnham Green on Route 55 which operated between Greenford and Chiswick as does its present day version numbered E3. Here the bus is only working as far as Northfields. (D.W.K.Jones)

In November what was once C1 was again operating for the LPTB, albeit now on loan from J.R.Manuel who traded as J.M.Coaches from Holloway. No alterations have been made to the body manufactured at Chiswick works and even the rear blind box has been put to good use for the vehicle's duties on Route 19 between Clapham Junction and Finsbury Park. Later the bus passed to Overland Lismore Coaches and yet again entered London Transport service this time on Route 68 as can be seen in the 1948 book of this series. Originally sold by the Board in November 1940, the smart normal control twenty seat bus was eventually to be withdrawn from passenger use on a permanent basis in June 1951. (V.C.Jones)

Against the familiar background of Windmill Lane, Greenford Bristol B1 lays over before departing on a journey which will take it to Brentford over a route which in years to come would be called E2. The Bristol K5G buses which entered service as B1 to B9 were the second batch of non-standard types to be allocated to the Board during the darkest days of the war. The very small diameter headlights were later replaced by larger units and the metal panel to the rear of the upper deck was later to be replaced by a glass window. Other than the replacement of a Gardner engine by an AEC 7.7 litre example later in their lives, these buses operated in much the same condition through to the early 1950s when they were all withdrawn from passenger service. (D.W.K.Jones)

PG7681 had a chequered career. It first entered service in April 1930 and was finally disposed of in May 1953. Starting as a Hall Lewis bodied 28 seat rear entrance private hire coach with the East Surrey Traction Co.Ltd. on 15th April 1930, it was first numbered T309 when Green Line Coaches Ltd. allocated fleet numbers to all coaches. In 1935 it was renumbered T393 when it was realised the earlier number was already carried by an ex-Tilling bus. In 1938 the body was removed and the chassis used in the construction of a tramway conduit flusher and the vehicle was then given service vehicle fleet number 113W. Here it is seen having just passed Merton garage making rather a mess and on a section of tram track where there is no conduit as such. Maybe it cleaned out the rails as well ensuring a smooth passage for the E/1 tram on Service 4 following in the distance on its journey to Victoria Embankment. (J.Lines collection)

Q72 from Crawley garage operates the long 434 route which skirted the southern boundary of the LPTB area from Horsham to Dormansland through Crawley and East Grinstead. This unbelievably tranquil scene is actually outside the 'White Hart' in Crawley and the properties behind the bus were to be demolished in due course as the last picture in the 1955 book of this series shows. The 4Q4 class went through several changes of seating arrangement, eventually becoming 35 seaters by the time this picture was taken. (S.E.Letts)

Croydon based ST189 has broken down while working duty TC11 on the southern section of Route 12 which operated between Oxford Circus and South Croydon, Red Deer. The conductor has propped the faretable board against the back of the bus as a signal to prevent other drivers pulling close up behind and some disconsolate passengers wait for the next 12 to come along. (V.C.Jones)

LT38 is about to depart from the terminus of Route 29 at Blanche Lane, South Mimms for a journey to Turnpike Lane Station on the northern section of this long standing route in the early part of the year. Only recently transferred in from Leyton in place of the new STDs rejected by Potters Bar garage, it was to give just over a year's service before two more garages, Upton Park and Muswell Hill, were to have the pleasure of operating the bus. The body, number 10324, was separated from the chassis in April 1949 and both parts then scrapped two months apart. (D.W.K.Jones)

'Bluebird' 60 seat LT1281 has pulled up well away from the kerb giving passengers a short walk to board the bus which is making its way to Mortlake on Route 9 in this view taken outside St.James', Piccadilly. Having first entered service in May 1932 it is nearing its permanent retirement from operation, being dispatched to Daniels of Rainham for scrap in August 1949. Although built as a 5LT6 this code changed in April 1934 when an oil engine was substituted for its petrol unit, becoming 11LT6/4. The double deck variety of the LT class bus was converted to diesel in the 1930s and by 1940 only the fifty four with Wilson gearboxes and 149 of the original open staircase examples remained in use with the older means of propulsion. (J.G.S.Smith collection)

D77 was one of only six to be delivered in red and white livery from the batch of Duple bodied 1/1D2/1 Daimlers numbered D74 to D92 delivered in 1945. The others were received in a brown livery. This class was first seen on the roads of London in 1944 courtesy of the Ministry of War Transport, who only authorised Bedford, Bristol, Daimler and Guy to manufacture passenger service vehicles during the latter years of the war. Gradually this class replaced all the STLs at Sutton and the majority at Merton with the last entering service in November 1946. This Merton garaged bus is working from Sutton garage on Route 80 heading for Tooting at Sutton Green. Such loans were not uncommon particularly at times of race meetings at Epsom. (A.B.Cross)

The long shadow of the raincoated photographer indicates late afternoon sunshine when Q59 was caught by the camera exiting Bakers Lane into Belmont Road at Uxbridge on Route 309. The blind indicates a short journey to Harefield and the two man crew seem to be the only occupants of this 35 seater bus. Why it should be carrying a WA garage plate is an unsolved mystery since the route was operated by WT with occasional help from MA and certainly not by WA who in the normal way of things did not operate 4Q4s. The bus itself was allocated to WT in 1947. (K.A.V.Newley collection)

TF84 stands in the shadows in Allsop Place behind Baker Street Station, having worked up from the country. The driver has reset the route blind for the return journey to Dorking on Route 714 before his disappearance for a well earned period of relaxation. In the distance a 10T10 is making its way to a convenient parking space behind the TF at this well used stand which for most of 1947 was used by coaches on Routes 709, 710, 711 and 714, until the first three routes were extended across London into Buckinghamshire in November. (S.A.Newman)

Amersham garage provided some additional buses for hospital traffic on Sundays on Route 309 between Harefield and Uxbridge Station (Und) and habitually used Green Line 10T10 coaches for the purpose. T672 is seen waiting at Uxbridge Station. These second generation of purpose built Green Line coaches had seen varied use during World War II and all excepting the small number which failed to return were to relive their pre-war experiences until replaced by the RF class in 1951 and 1952. (L.T.P.S.)

Lead bus LT522 operates from Old Kent Road garage while LT401, a Plumstead vehicle, is parked behind at West End Green, West Hampstead on Route 53A. The notice fixed below the running numbers advises the public of the fact that 53A buses will not be seen in this part of London for much longer. On 12th November the 53A swopped northern terminals with 59, 59A and 159 and thereafter journeyed north of Oxford Circus to Camden Town instead. Interestingly the higher numbered bus is diesel powered while the other has a petrol engine in combination with a Wilson preselective gearbox giving potential riders a much quieter and more pleasant ride. Plumstead garage was always the home for the residual petrol engined double deck LTs fitted with this type of transmission and which carried a variety of bodies from the basic LT3, LT5 and LT6 types.

With Queen Elizabeth's Hunting Lodge behind, LT384 of Leyton garage waits on the stand at the Royal Forest Hotel, Chingford while the crew and an inspector converse with each other. Doubtless working Route 38, although from this angle no proof of this can be seen, this LT is typical of the stock used to work the fairly long run to Victoria in 1947. This example has a 'camel back' body - so called because of the profile of the front blind box being set into the cab roof. When first delivered a route board was fitted above the box and a few years later the rather quaint light was fitted above. By 1947 these features had fallen out of use. (A.B.Cross)

The bright sunlight shows up the rivets and blemishes on LT888 as it stands at the Croydon Airport terminus of Route 194. The fixing clips for the route board above the blind box are still in place although they will not have been used for at least seven years. Whether Fynnon Salt really did much for rheumatism is debatable but this type of medical claim was still very prevalent in advertising at the time. Eventually this bus was to meet the same fate as the majority of the class being scrapped in December 1948. (J.Gascoine collection)

LT1305, seen taking a well earned rest from its duties on Route 148 at Leytonstone, Green Man, shows that body number 13124 has considerable deterioration with signs of bulge and sag above the rear wheels. Even with these shortcomings the bus had to soldier on until May 1949 when at last it would be scrapped by R.L.Daniels of Rainham. (R.Burrell)

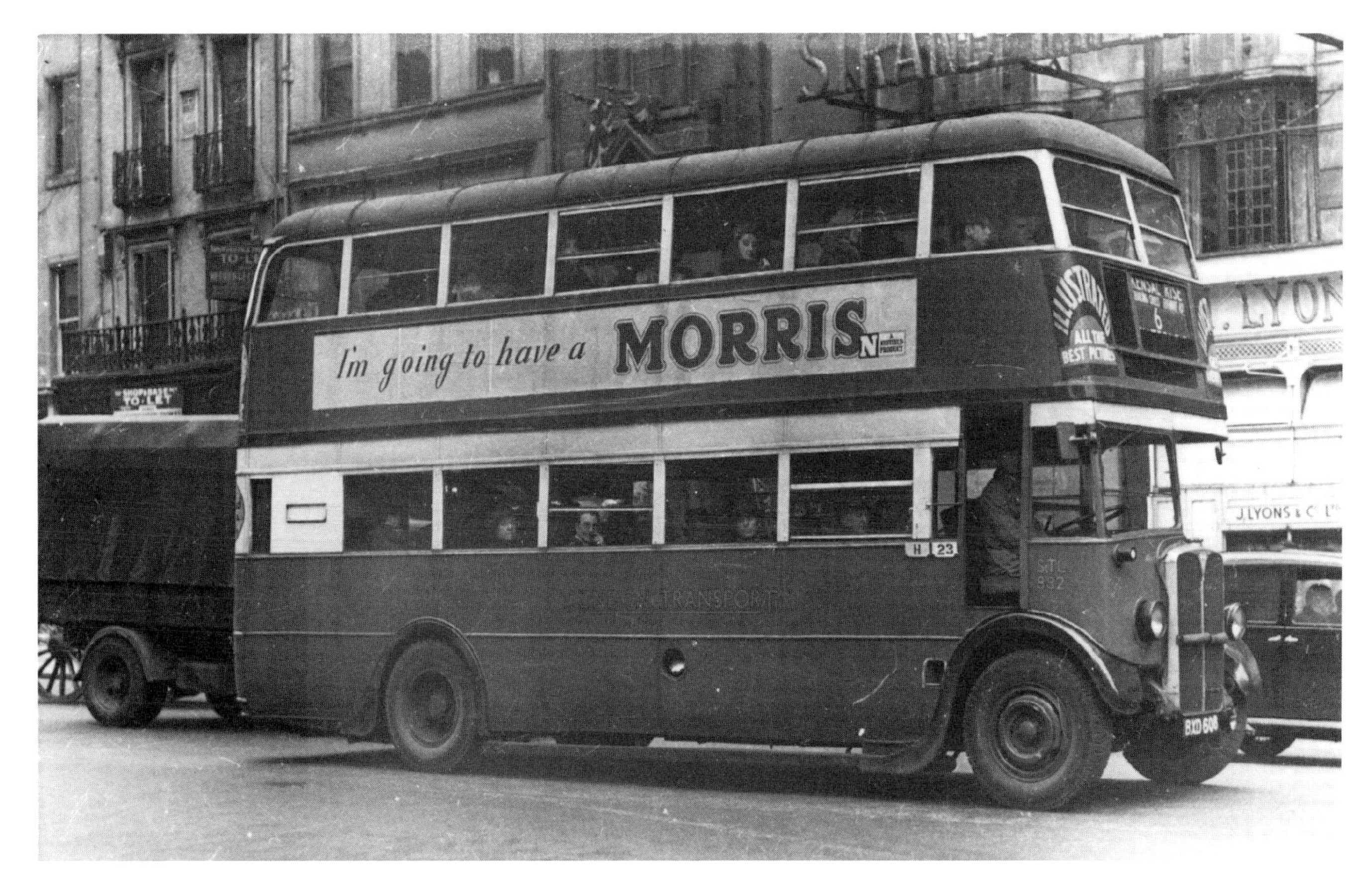

The advertisement on the side of STL882 is as much aimed at lifting the depressed post-war spirits as selling new cars, given the long waiting lists for the limited output available for sale. The restricted windows of the J.Lyons teashop are still displaying the results of war damage and add to the period feel of this view taken as this Hackney bus makes its way along the Strand on Route 6 to Kensal Rise. Both body and chassis date from 1935 although the body, number 15292 of STL5 type, was carried by STL1067 when it first entered service from Merton garage. The combination seen here came together in February 1939 and it so remained until being withdrawn from service in December 1950 for scrap. (Omnibus Society)

With passenger entrance right at the front of the vehicle forward of the wheels and directly opposite the driver's compartment, Q113, one of the 5Q5 variety, would have made an ideal OMO bus but the entire batch always saw use as two person operated vehicles, at least during their London Transport service. Bodywork is of all metal construction built by Park Royal for 37 passengers. During the wartime a number had their seating altered to 33 to allow for more standing passengers but all were reconverted over a lengthy period starting in November 1945 and again in February 1949. The finish to the interior is to the specific requirements called for by the LPTB and closely resembles products built at their own works at the time. Certain features such as arm rests on the longitudinal seat directly above the power unit; curtain to the open side of the driver's cab and fareboard clipped in position below the front windscreen - in this case for Route 200 - are noteworthy. (V.C.Jones)

Some effort was made in certain quarters to provide proper blinds for odd vehicles. Here ex-Tilling ST882 carries a blind made for its use from Leyton garage. Interestingly the old chestnut of how to spell this particular destination has raised its head. By 1947 the accepted spelling was High Beach but this compiler obviously had a conception of trees in Epping Forest! Through the lower deck windows a number of what appears to be withdrawn LTs can be seen with route blinds removed and in September 1948 this ST would be joining them eventually to be scrapped in December of the same year. (D.W.K.Jones)

Among the recipients of the post-war STD batch of sixty five buses of all Leyland construction, Potters Bar garage staff soon became dissatisfied with them and elected to keep older types in service until the arrival of the post-war RTs. STD146, after being initially operated by PB for a couple of weeks, was transferred to Loughton to further enhance their allocation. The 38A route was added to the 10A on which the Leylands were already in use. The bus is seen in Epping Town heading south to Leytonstone as duty L23 in 'as new' condition. (C.Carter)

The Permanent Way Engineer at Lillie Bridge Depot is the current custodian of khaki liveried 442W, alias the chassis of T175 with a new service fleet body number 9167. This total picture evokes a period long since passed with the white rings to the road bollards, some unifying decorative brickwork to the background buildings which nevertheless show a measure of modification over the years. In October 1963 the vehicle also passed into history being disposed of to a Mr.W.McMann of Barnet, the chassis having been in the ownership of London Transport and its predecessors since September 1930. (J.Lines collection)

Careful inspection of the opening window arrangement and lack of a radius finish to the corners of the non-opening windows suggests that much remodelling has taken place on this LGOC body, number 12209, since its manufacture. Originally carried on ST664 it now graces the chassis of ST38 and carries duty plates P4 while resting in Finsbury Square before departing south on Route 21. Note too the unusual treatment of the rear offside lower deck corner which appears to be painted red. (J.Gascoine collection)

Two members of the 18STL20 batch, STL2684 the lead bus and both with identical advertising, stand parked at the Uxbridge terminus of Route 321 against a background which is completely transformed nowadays. Both buses have had their early style of route blinds with three intermediate points reset for the return journey to Luton. Upon the first overhaul programme of these provincial looking additions to the STL class they would emerge from Chiswick in a slightly altered paint scheme which can be seen in books covering later years in this series. (M.Rooum)

LT1042 has set down its passengers on arrival at Muswell Hill Broadway on route 244 and the driver has reset the blind for the next journey to Winchmore Hill, Chase Side Tavern. Although journeys had travelled beyond this destination to the Capitol Cinema from October 1943 and fixed stopping places were introduced between Chase Side Tavern and Green Lanes in March 1944, it was not until the year under review that a regular daily service was provided through to the Capitol. In the opposite direction a pre-war Wolseley saloon glides away on the damp surface. Typical of the period hats are well in evidence, the traffic is light, there are no parked cars or indeed yellow lines and some shop fronts still require attention from the glazier. (A.B.Cross)

This bus, T234, first entered service in January 1931 as a petrol engined Duple bodied coach, being garaged at Alpha Street, Slough. With the delivery of the improved 10T10 coaches in 1938 and 1939, this coach together with the entire batch made up of T207 to T306 were withdrawn from Green Line work, the last in March 1939. Twenty six of these coaches were converted to 11T11 configuration with fairly new Weymann bodies which had been used to breathe new life into some of the R class AEC Reliances. T234 was one of those converted, now carrying the body first mounted on R8 and in between very temporarily fitted on to the chassis of T367. Still with brown painted roof and now defunct roof mounted sidelights it operates from Harrow Weald garage, having been repainted into Central Area livery in January 1946. The 221 route from North Harrow to Pinner via Hatch End was HD's only single deck route at the time and ran into Pinner via Paines Lane, a road that even today's ubiquitous minibuses fail to serve. (J.G.S.Smith collection)

Traffic lights control the traffic heading towards Haymarket but that entering Piccadilly Circus from Regent Street is still unhindered by such restraints in this view taken on 5th August. Various types of bus and one coach thread their way round Eros on their journeys to their respective destinations. Middle Row's STL399 in the centre operates Route 15 as far as Aldgate not venturing into the East End section of the route. Other buses work routes 6, 9 and 22 while the Green Line T class coach is in service on Route 709 to Godstone having commenced its journey at Baker Street. A number of pedestrians make their way across the wide roadway in haphazard fashion, not unduly bothered by the relatively light traffic. (L.T.Museum U40503)

Square cabbed ST1092 on temporary loan to Grays from Hertford garage is seen in company with ST167 which, having been repainted into green Country Area colours in October 1945, spent its remaining operational life mostly at Grays. On this wet and dismal day the ex-East Surrey Traction Company ST is ready for use on Route 374 which operated between Grays and Uplands Estate. (J.G.S.Smith collection)

D161 is viewed at Aldgate in the two shades of green livery for its use on the heavily trafficked Green Line services provided by Romford, London Road garage. This route had in pre-war years, when known as Y2, been operated by single deckers. These Daimler built chassis incorporated AEC engines and the bodies were manufactured by Duple to a relaxed utility design with normal seating for 56 passengers. The complete vehicle was coded 4/1D2/3 when new. Ready to depart from Aldgate on the full service through to Corbets Tey as duty number 41, the bus displays the newer black on yellow blinds. (L.T.P.S.)

It is not certain why it was necessary to paint 'Low Loader' on the driver's air vent cover of D5 seen waiting at Morden Underground station before departing on a circuit of the 127 route which will finish with a run in to its home garage. The arrival of these Daimler CWA6 models with Duple bodywork for 55 seated passengers started in May 1944 and were a direct result of the Ministry of Supply allowing a quota of this type of double decker to be built. Previously they had viewed that normal height buses provided a more economical use of labour when compared to the special requirements needed to produce a small number of reduced height vehicles. In another twist of fate it was in 1943 that other bodybuilders which had been approached could not meet the required needs of the Board and thirteen Guy Arab chassis allocated for lowbridge bodies never materialised. This picture, taken on 26th April, gives a clear view of the unusual ventilators fitted above the nearside bulkhead saloon window, a feature hidden in shadow in most photographs. (L.Housden collection)

Route 237, then numbered 137, was first operated by little Dennis Darts of varying seating capacity from 17 to 20 seats at the time LPTB was formed in 1933 and the route also saw service from C1, the prototype Leyland Cub. 20 seat Leyland Cubs took over operations in December 1939 and then on 7th December 1942 the route was upgraded with crew operated single deck LTs seating 35 passengers. The route was always worked from Hounslow garage in its single deck days and LT1050 is pictured alongside its home base as it departs for Chertsey Station on duty AV8.

Two elderly coaches, numbered 6 and 7 by A.J.Roberts, the proprietor of Ashford Belle Coaches are seen parked in between their peak hour use on Route 65. The AEC's VH registration indicates it was registered in Huddersfield prior to 1936 but from a London point of view the Gilford Hera coach CNO76 is the more interesting. This originated in June 1935 with Hillman's Airways, the aviation off-shoot of the well known East London coach operator. It was even fitted with a specially strengthened bullion compartment at the rear. It passed to British Airways and then BOAC before ending up with Mr.Roberts. The Wycombe built body is recorded as only seating 24 passengers. The coach ended its days as a showman's bus at Ringwood in the New Forest. (A.B.Cross)

In March 1949 the LTs which had served Route 122 faithfully since its inauguration on 9th September 1936 would begin to be replaced by new RTL class vehicles. Here for the present LT1238, fitted with a petrol engine and Wilson preselective gearbox, waits on the stand at Thomas Street, Woolwich. The radio shop offers an accumulator charging service, something unheard of today but necessary for many in 1947 if they wished to enjoy BBC radio programmes. (A.B.Cross)

STL2680, an 'unfrozen' STL of 1942 vintage, pauses outside its home garage of Godstone en-route from West Croydon to East Grinstead on Route 409. For an explanation of the term 'unfrozen' readers are referred to the introduction to the 1939/45 book of this series. East Grinstead is the present day southern terminus of Route 409 but in 1947 most journeys ran on to Forest Row, although this journey is not going that far. STL2680 first entered service at Watford High Street for a very brief period with three others of the batch after which they were all moved to Godstone who also took some of those which had previously been in service from High Wycombe and Amersham. Ideally suited for hill climbing because of their gearbox, clutch and differential ratio they were soon in use on Routes 409 and 411 which climbed Church Hill at Caterham. (M.Rooum)

STL1051 has appeared twice before in this series of books. In the 1939/45 volume it can be seen with wartime accoutrements and in the 1953 book it is seen in its twilight days in Garston garage. Here it waits at Godstone for a crew change while working its 'natural' route, 410 from Reigate to Bromley. The valances to the non-opening windows have now been removed and a plain panel has replaced the glass in the first bay immediately next to the driver's cab door. It has still to gain the post-war County Area colour scheme and be relieved of all its glass louvres. (P.J.Marshall)

From February Leyton garage used RT38, first as a type trainer and later in service, to familiarise the staff in readiness for the forthcoming delivery of the post-war RTs. It is seen here deserted at Woodford Bridge with duty plates T13 prior to its journey to Victoria on the first route to be equipped with RT3s. After a spell at this garage it moved on to Potters Bar and before the end of the year had reached Bromley, in each case fulfiling the same function. RT52 was the bus which performed similar duties at Croydon garage in readiness for their allocation of a small number which replaced post-war STDs.

Green Line liveried T590 works as NF57 on bus route 450, the 'scenic route' between Gravesend and Dartford. In common with many new vehicle deliveries of the pre-war era, registration numbers and fleet numbers were allocated in advance to give numerical sequence coupled to the chassis numbers. The body fitted gave a much more accurate date of when the complete vehicle emerged from Chiswick ready for service as indicated by the body number carried. Hence this coach entered service in July 1938 together with thirty four identical examples which carried numbers in the range T499 to T605. Upon its return from military service with the U.S. forces stationed in England, this coach spent sometime in Chiswick Works before re-emerging once again for the use for which it was originally built, entering service at Northfleet on 1st June 1946. (W.J.Haynes)

Forty nine Guy Arab II chassis fitted with Massey bodywork were delivered to the Board between May and September 1945 all being in a livery of two shades of brown with no light colour relief except for the last six which were delivered in light brown and broken white. G184 is flanked by ST149 nearest the camera and LT245 furthest away, all having just received attention from the craftsmen at Chiswick in November. G184 was one of the first to be repainted into traditional red and white. It is surprising to see the dents on both the ST and the Guy which appear to have just been painted over. Equally interesting are the five different Michelin tyre advertisements carried on the three vehicles. The white finished stanchions fitted to the Guy and its angular appearance present a most uncompromising image. (L.T.Museum U41277)

Twenty years separates the entry into service of LT1142 and TD9 photographed while resting from their duties on Route 210 on Golders Green station forecourt. A considerable difference is shown in the liveries carried by the two Central Area operated buses. The delivery of the batch of Weymann bodied Ts, 719-768, in the first half of 1946 introduced the all red with narrow cream band livery to the single deck fleet and this was to continue on all future deliveries of new Central Area single deckers as shown by the TD which entered service in the last month of 1946. Miraculously the LT still retains three of its glass storm valances. (L.T.P.S.)

ST591 was a long time resident of Catford garage. It is seen here at West Croydon Station before departing for Woolwich by way of Route 75 while the gentleman in the Homburg hat eyes the photographer with suspicion. The bus is in its final form as a 1ST1/1 with body number 11423, which had been built by the LGOC and first mounted on the chassis of ST455. This was the last winter of public use for the bus which was withdrawn from service in May 1948 and scrapped in the following month. (A.B.Cross)

The fact that the fleet in 1947 was still in poor state is reflected by at least two pictures in this book showing broken down vehicles. CR16b in green livery has made it round the roundabout at the Malden Road intersection with the main A3 London to Portsmouth arterial road but that is as far as it got and now it awaits the arrival of the breakdown van. The six wheeled bus travelling in the opposite direction is LT1062, the normal type of work horse on this route and the rear view shows it is carrying one of the first batch of bodies which lacked a rear destination blind. Although a 213 number stencil is carried, the display of a destination board has ceased, although some garages, notably Croydon and Elmers End did continue to use them. (A.B.Cross)

ST941 rescued from the training fleet has quickly been put to work from Northfleet garage on Route 480 operating between Gravesend and Dartford as the makeshift route board proclaims. In this view taken on 24th May at Gravesend the ST is parked in front of STL1494 representing the more usual type of vehicle employed on this route. There is plenty of body sag in evidence between the wheelbase of this ex-Tilling ST which was withdrawn from service in October 1948 to be scrapped in the early months of the following year. (V.C.Jones)

Wartime utility construction is exemplified in this rear view of Park Royal bodied G26. A panelled emergency rear exit to the upper deck; lack of any destination and route equipment either on this elevation or to the side; the basic outline of the roof dome and the white painted disc all shout utility. A passenger approaching from the adjacent Victoria Station would need to walk to the front to establish the route this Guy Arab might be working although regulars could have an educated guess. This particular bus was always garaged at Tottenham and is standing on the time honoured space for Route 76 vehicles. Note the faded white paintwork on the kerb. (J.Lines collection)

The prototype RT body is now carried on the chassis of RT19 having reached its newer underframe in December 1945 and is viewed here at the Putney Heath terminus of Route 74. The loss of the staircase window and repositioned route number plate holder are evident in this offside view though this work had been carried out while the body was still mounted on its original chassis. Temporarily lacking a rear wheel disc and painted in the post-war livery later adopted as standard, nobody at the time could have envisaged that this body would still be in evidence some fifty years plus after first being built. (V.C.Jones)

If 'Little Ben' is keeping good time LT67 has just departed at 13.55 from Victoria Station on its journey to Chingford on Route 38. It will turn left into Victoria Street before making its way to Hyde Park Corner and Piccadilly and eventually northwards to its destination just inside Epping Forest. The sixteen year old body of composite construction shows its age with clearly identifiable sag along its length but with the shortage of new buses it had to soldier on, still operating from Leyton garage until May 1949 when it made its final journey to Daniels of Rainham. (S.A.Newman)

The Rainham War Memorial terminus finds Hornchurch garaged G219 waiting to take up duties for its journey to Havering Park, Clockhouse Lane by way of Route 165. In service with London Transport between July 1945 and June 1951, just six short years, its new owners the Atomic Energy Research Establishment at Harwell managed to obtain nearly eight years use from this Guy Arab II chassis with NCME bodywork. (A.B.Cross)

Victoria garage's STL2520 about to depart for Woodford Bridge on Route 10. Although the trees in Grosvenor Gardens seem yet to gain their leaves and the pedestrians look well wrapped up, the driver is wearing his summer white coat. In 1947, after the harsh winter, spring was obviously late in arriving. The bus carries an LPTB built body which represented the final major development for the STL class and the complete vehicle was given the code 15STL16. Around six months after this STL was delivered the first production 2RT2s were entering service. By 1947 the distinctive deep radiator has been replaced by the more dumpy standard STL type, a narrower life guard rail has replaced that originally fitted and the bus has lost its rear wheel disc. In 1948 the chassis of this bus was modified and reappeared as SRT2, as can be seen in the picture that appears in the 1949 book of this series, while the body was used to replace the Park Royal version carried by STL2072. (K.A.V.Newley collection)

On 7th August, with the rolling landscape of the Kent countryside as a background, T683 climbs the North Downs on the southern leg of its journey through to Windsor while in service on Route 704. Very little exists in the way of road markings and there do not appear to be any cats eyes to help drivers in the hours of darkness. The fence on the left is all there is to prevent an errant vehicle from plunging through the trees and down the escarpment. (L.T.Museum U40580)

From this vantage point the six roof ventilators on STL103 can be clearly seen as it makes its way to Oxford Circus on Croydon's allocation on Route 12. Additional ventilation for the lower deck was provided with three apertures on each side of the bus immediately above the windows. The roof is now painted brown with LPTB red and broken white as the main colours and is a far cry from the Tilling standard dark red, cream lower deck waist band and upper saloon window frames with silver roof in which the bus first entered service in March 1933. Another significant change is the loss of the single route number box which was originally fitted above the platform. This was removed at the time of the vehicle's first overhaul and replaced by a metal stencil holder at the base of the rearmost lower deck window. By now this has been moved to the top of the same window to better catch the back lighting from within the saloon at night. (L.Housden collection)

Recently delivered RT407, the first Weymann bodied example to be allocated to Croydon garage, purrs along Streatham High Road on 12th October. The tortuous South London Route 115 was a surprising early recipient of new RTs, believed to be as a result of Croydon driver's difficulties in matching the performance of the relatively new Daimlers which Sutton put out on the route. The tram tracks, street furniture and traffic - or lack of it - portray a Streatham High Road aeons away from the present day scene. (J.H.Price)

Merton Road, Southfields is the location of this photograph of STL281 which has just commenced a run on Route 39 from the Station to Camden Town. The order for the batch of one hundred STLs from STL253 to 352 was actually placed by LPTB in the Board's first month of existence, July 1933, although the groundwork had already been completed by the LGOC. Here the bus is carrying body number 13719 which was matched to the chassis of STL286 when new in December 1933. After several interim changes it settled on STL281 in September 1939 and remained there until scrapped in May 1950. (C.Carter)

ST1101 is pictured on the stand in the lay-by off Wood Street, Kingston which was an additional terminal facility provided in the previous year. Four routes used this stand and ST1101 is seen as it rests between duties to and from Little Bookham, Preston Cross by way of Route 418. One other Country Area service, the 406, together with Central Area Routes 131 and 216 commenced their journeys here. An STL, probably on the 406, is parked near the entrance to the lay-by. Bentalls' advertisements are prominent on both vehicles. (A.B.Cross)

Piccadilly Circus looking towards Regent Street on 11th June reveals four STLs, five LTs and a Green Line T class coach among a variety of other interesting vehicles negotiating the statue of Eros, the Greek God of Love. Other notable landmarks are the Swan & Edgar's store building on the left and the County Fire Office to the right while in between the line of Nash's Quadrant leading into Regent Street is legacy of the great replanning of this part of London in the early 19th century. While the traffic is not of present day grid lock proportions it is noticeable that the two LTs on the right of the picture are both heading for Clapham Common on Route 88 - nominally a six to eight minute service. (L.T.Museum U40167)

The additional bonnet length required to house the Gardner 6LW engine in the batch of LT class vehicles numbered LT1417 to LT1426 is clearly evident in this view of LT1419. The batch were allocated to Hanwell garage from November 1932 until the end of 1946. In 1947 several were allocated to Grays garage where LT1419 is seen ready for duty on Route 371A. This particular bus was refitted with an AEC diesel engine in December 1947 then being transferred to Upton Park.

Petrol engined ST and LT class vehicles were a common sight in the immediate post-war years acting in the capacity of learner vehicles. Here, standing beside the Victoria garage building, ST926 is the current training vehicle for that garage, while LT76 parked behind was used for around four months commencing in the early summer by West Green garage in the same role. No doubt the trainees and instructors are enjoying a canteen break using the fine facilities provided as a necessary part of all London Transport designed and built garages. Both vehicles were subsequently returned to passenger use before ending their careers with the Executive in 1948. It is worthy of note that the fuel tanks are carried on opposite sides of these two vehicles both manufactured by AEC and entering service in 1930. (D.W.K.Jones)

What memories this picture of Tottenham's long serving LT872 evokes as it stands at the head of a line of 73s in Richmond Bus Station in the late afternoon. A good load of passengers have taken their seats, snatches of conversation can be heard, odd swirls of tobacco smoke eddy around the upper deck and the timbers of the fourteen year old vehicle creak a little in the warmth of the unaccustomed winter sunshine. Soon the crew will appear, the bus will sway as the driver climbs into the cab; a whine from the starter motor and the engine splutters into life; the conductor gives two bells and slowly the bus edges into Richmond, turns its back on the sun and takes its patient passengers along Sheen Road towards town.

During the period of restricted blinds, Country Area STLs continued to use the separate route number blind where one was available. This enabled a much smaller aperture on the other box to accommodate the lengthy blinds required at some garages. For example, the Watford High Street blind required 49 different exposures. STL981b leaves Uxbridge Station for Windsor Castle on Route 457A in the late afternoon low angled sunlight which seems to emphasise the draughty front entrance provided. LPTB bodied the first batch of STLs built to this configuration which represented the initial large scale replacement of earlier variants of double deckers that had formed the basis of the Country Area when LPTB was formed on 1st July 1933. (K.A.V.Newley collection)

The date is 26th April and with a background of trees beginning to break out into their spring foliage, STL1466b journeys to East Grinstead on Route 409. The Weymann bodies carried by this final batch of front entrance STL class buses numbering fifty in total were of all metal construction and were reckoned to be of superior quality to the earlier LPTB built batch of eighty nine STLs in similar configuration. (L.Housden collection)

The lower panelling of the ex-Tilling STs did not reach the level of their LGOC contemporaries and therefore a two tiered life guard was fitted. This allowed much more of the underbody to come into view and the offside extra long rectangular shaped fuel tank can easily be seen on ST887. As with ST906 shown later in this book it is seen while in use on the special Epsom racecourse route operating between Epsom Station and the Downs but in this instance the route number is incorrectly displayed as 406E, which pedantically was the service from Epsom Town rather than the Station which should be 406F. Away from London between January 1942 and May 1944, Stockton Corporation had the dubious task of operating this petrol engined open staircase AEC Regent of 1930 vintage. (J.G.S.Smith collection)

Tilling numbered their short AEC Regents for London use in the series 6013 through to 6198. They were fitted with open staircase bodies in either their own coachwork factories situated at Lewisham, Camberwell and Brighton or by Dodson. These 186 vehicles received LPTB fleet numbers ST837 to ST1022 and a further five identical vehicles transferred from Tilling's Brighton operations numbered 6255/7/8/30/6 were renumbered ST1023 to ST1027. All were coded 2ST7 or 1/2ST7. Initially ST989 carried fleet number 6165. In its twilight years this bus is seen operating on Route 12 from Nunhead garage heading for Dulwich Library. (S.A.Newman)

All over brown liveried G313 working from Enfield garage passes through Muswell Hill Broadway on its journey to Chingford by way of Route 102 sometime in September. Massey bodywork is carried, 59 such bodies being fitted to Guy Arab chassis for London Transport, who did not have much say in the combination of chassis and body they would be allocated by the Government. A picture of this bus appears in the 1952 book of this series after it had received a normal paint scheme. My colleague David Ruddom tells me that throughout the war and when this picture was taken his family shopped in the Lipton's branch behind the bus and two doors up Martyn's shop had a coffee roasting machine in the window which filled the street with a beautiful aroma for many years.

ST17 arrives at Kingston on Richmond Road on its way to Leatherhead as duty K2 while in use on Route 65. Rather unusually at this late date the vehicle retains its glass window pane on the lower deck by the staircase. These had been replaced by panels in the interests of modesty on most of the LT and ST class of vehicle many years previous. This bus was a long time servant of Kingston and remained there until it made its last journey to Daniels for scrap in 1949. (A.B.Cross)

ST993 works the circular route 243 which at this time was operated by Old Kent Road garage using STs during the week and LTs on a Sunday. An ex-Tilling ST, albeit with very good blinds, was more unusual however. Between May 1942 and February 1944 this bus had been on loan to Red & White Motor Services of Chepstow. Upon its return and after a short spell in store, it reappeared mainly as a learner vehicle until the acute vehicle shortage prevailing in the period necessitated its return to public service. The rather dejected queue were probably glad to see the bus arrive despite its age considering that the weather looks very damp and the well shuttered Jones and Higgins store on Rye Lane precluded any idle window shopping to pass the time. (Omnibus Society)

A sturdy pre-war Leyland Cheetah waits on the Clapham Junction stand of Route 19 before a journey to Finsbury Park. Now in the possession of J.M.Motors of Holloway, it carries a London registration, although so far details of its original owner have eluded the author. The standard red telephone boxes, now a heritage item, show no signs of vandalism as befits the ordered society of 1947. (D.A.Ruddom collection)

Ex-T351 was fitted in October 1935 with this Weymann 29 seat front entrance body, very similar to those which finished up on the 11T11s. It is almost unaltered when photographed in Douai, France over twenty years on from its transformation to bus status. When it first entered service in April 1930 with Blue Belle Motors Ltd. of London, operators of excursions and an express route between Paddington and East Grinstead, a London Lorries 31 seat coach body was carried. The express route and six vehicles, given numbers T346 to T351, were taken over by Green Line on 20th July 1932. The bus last saw service for a couple weeks in June 1944 at Windsor garage before being stored at Potters Bar garage prior to disposal in May 1945. (J.H.Price)

Austerity displayed at Wembley, Empire Pool in the form of G370, B23 and B28. From left to right the Weymann bodied Guy is one of only three HGC registered examples operated by Alperton garage while the two Hanwell based Bristols with Duple bodies are from the second batch carrying similar index letters. All three vehicles are actually of a more relaxed austerity style than were earlier members of their classes with five opening windows to each side being provided together with a side blind box. Nevertheless the luxury of the RT family was yet to come. Note the different sized headlights supplied by the two chassis manufacturers. (D.W.K.Jones)

This combination of a Leyland SKPZ2 chassis with Park Royal 20 seat body painted in a sky blue and cream livery epitomises coach travel between the main line railway termini of London from 1936 to 1942 and 1946 until 1950. Unfortunately these stylish vehicles were replaced by standard RT class buses in their normal red livery with the loss of this characteristic batch of eight vehicles. The unwelcome break in their use on the Inter Station service was when they were on loan to ENSA, the acronym for the wartime Entertainments National Service Association, which provided light entertainment to the armed forces. Here C107 is seen in an incredibly peaceful terminus.

In 1947, as seen elsewhere in this book, Route 10 gained pre-eminence when the first post-war RTs were introduced on it by Leyton garage. Gillingham Street garage's weekday contribution to the route included STLs and STDs and STD130 waits on the stand at Victoria Station ready for a journey to Woodford Bridge. (L.T.P.S.)

CR5, still with white painted step to the saloon, looks suspiciously as if it has broken down in Parliament Square as it sits in the roadway with no human contact. It carries duty plates AL36 for its use on Route 88 to Mitcham normally operated by D class vehicles from Merton garage or LTs from Hammersmith. Even 20 seats would be missed by waiting passengers further along the route in these early post-war years of unreliability and non-appearance of scheduled buses. (J.G.S.Smith collection)

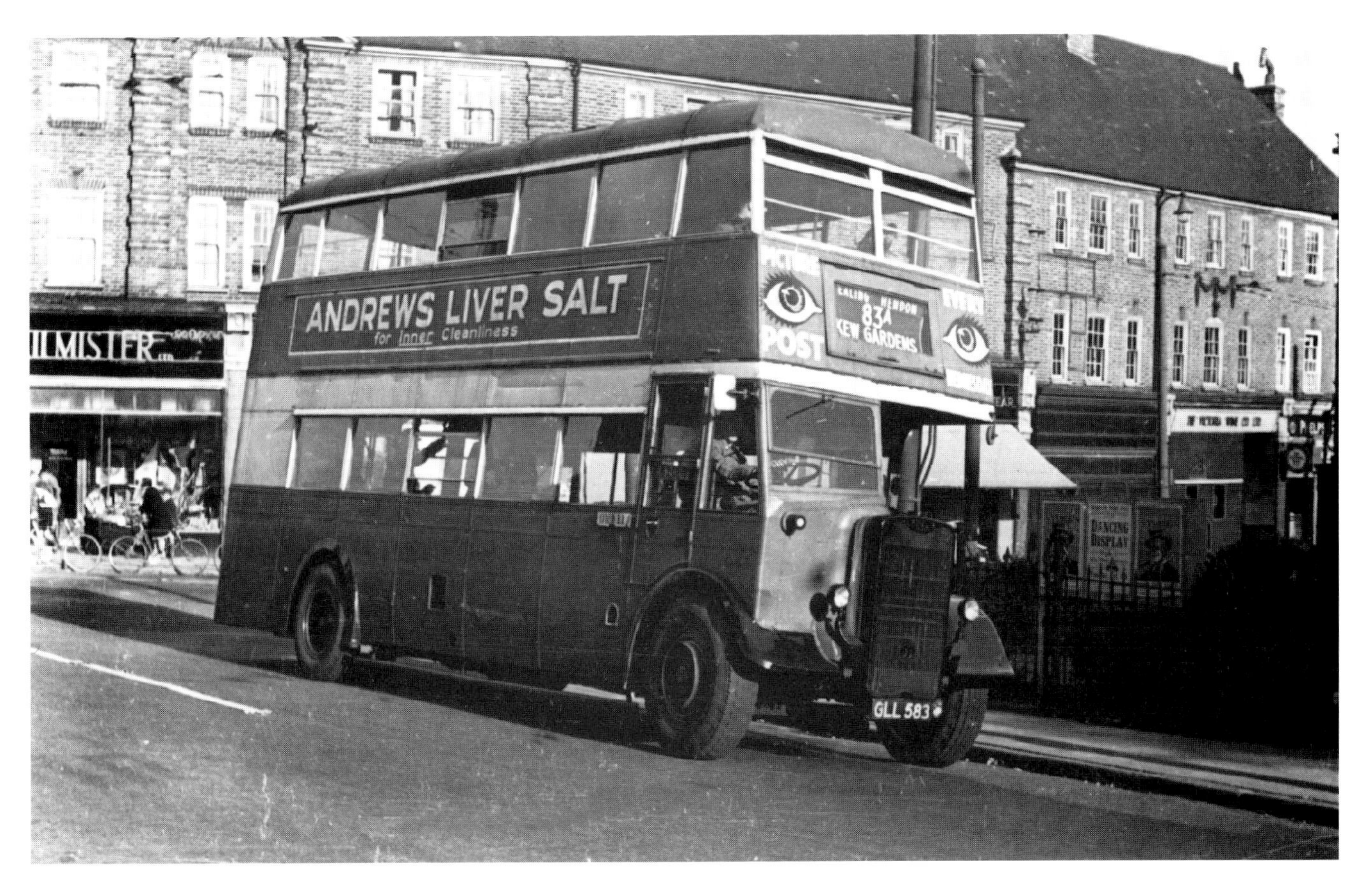

Park Royal bodied G83 had entered service in October 1943 from Alperton garage and was to be owned by London Transport for nine years before being disposed of to the South Western Omnibus Co. of Ceylon. Here at Wembley Triangle it is engaged on Route 83A. This was a Sunday only service first introduced on 24th May 1937 providing the variant south of Ealing to Kew Gardens over many years. The trolleybus wiring for the short working turn on Route 662 can be seen. This was chiefly used when events were taking place at Wembley Stadium and the destination was described on the blinds as 'STADIUM, Wembley Hill Road'. (S.A.Newman)

G204 has been pictured after sale to Highland Omnibuses in the 1954 book of this series and here it is seen in its earlier years while garaged at Hornchurch. This Park Royal bodied Guy Arab II, which entered service in September 1945, was always garaged at RD until its withdrawal and eventual disposal in November 1951 directly to its new owner north of the Border. Classified as a 1/3G8 at the time of delivery it was reclassified, along with many of the class to 1/3G8/1 later in its career and at present the author has been unable to establish why this occurred. (D.A.Jones)

During its short lived existence in 1932 the London General Country Services acquired twenty three new short wheelbase AEC Regents with bodies built by their parent LGOC of similar style to the so called 'Bluebird' LTs. When passed to the LPTB in 1933 they were classified 2ST4. Interestingly eight of the batch had three letter registrations, the only STs to carry this type if one disregards ST1140 which operated for a few months carrying EYK396. ST1033 is seen towards the end of its life operating from Watford High Street garage on Route 346 to Kingswood. WA was its final operational base before being withdrawn in December 1948 and scrapped in early 1949. (S.L.Poole)

Sidcup garage received green liveried T297 in October, it having moved into the Central Area in November 1946. After moving on from SP six months later it alternated between the Country and Central Areas for its last years of passenger use rather as an unwanted necessity. Standing at the Chislehurst terminus of Route 228 it will soon depart for Eltham, Well Hall Station on a route which at the time also saw single deck LTs and Qs. (W.J.Haynes)

With bright sunshine filtering through the trees, Alperton's G102 makes one of its Sunday and Bank Holiday trips south of the river on Route 72 to Esher. Having first entered service in January 1944 this Guy Arab II remained at ON until April 1951 when it made its only transfer to Barking. Withdrawn in February 1952 and acquired by L.W.Vass of Ampthill in September of that year it was to spend a longer period in use as a store shed in this Bedfordshire dealer's yard than it had done in passenger service, eventually being reduced to scrap in 1969. (A.B.Cross)

KJ2578 has a history stretching back to 1931 when it entered service with Redcar Services of Tunbridge Wells as a Weymann double deck bus with seating for 48 passengers. Together with a number of other Leyland vehicles it passed to Maidstone & District Motor Services Ltd. in February 1935. On 31st July 1935 the express service between Tunbridge Wells and London and the stage service from Sevenoaks to Tonbridge were acquired by the LPTB together with nine buses including this vehicle which received fleet number TD193. Withdrawn from service in 1939 it eventually was acquired by Liverpool Corporation via Millburn Motors, the Preston dealer. It lasted in revenue use until 1944 when it was first used as a learner vehicle and later rebuilt as a mobile canteen. It is seen in this capacity in St.Thomas Street, Liverpool with little to show its previous ancestry. (J.G.E.Nye)

Route 18B started life in July 1930 as Route 518 which followed the core 18 road but turned off at Wembley to run up to Preston Road. In June 1931 it was re-routed at Stonebridge Park to serve the newly opened North Circular Road as far as Finchley (Memorial). In the renumbering of October 1934 it became 18B and as such in 1947 provided the weekday service on the old 18 route south of Stonebridge Park. ST vehicles along with some STLs were the usual performers from Willesden Garage and here ST582 with duty plates AC14 makes its way to London Bridge. This was one of the last normal height STs to be withdrawn from service in 1950. (A.B.Cross)

Time appears to have stood still for the lady whose costume looks extremely antiquated even for 1947. Unless she is a ghost, she appears to have squeezed between the two STs on Route 16 at Victoria Station forecourt. ST744 shows its characteristic LGOC inherited fitting of rather oversized sidelights which LPTB continued specifying until wartime measures dictated smaller diameter fitments. During the war Wilts & Dorset Motor Service had the loan of this petrol engined AEC Regent with LGOC bodywork. The short wheelbase and straight staircase arrangement meant the standard ST only seated 49 passengers and this one first entered service in London during February 1931. (L.T.P.S.)

This photograph of LT316 shows small differences in its general appearance when compared to the view of the bus in later years which appeared in the 1950 book of this series. Metallic finish to the radiator surround and complete driver's nearside stalk adorn the vehicle as it journeys on Route 105 to Shepherds Bush. The mystery of the particular body code of this LGOC 56 seat body still remains. Built as a prototype for the later LT5 series with prominent inward curvature to the upper deck but with older type destination box, it was given body code LT4 according to the introduction of the PSV Circle publication dealing with the class. Later in the same work it is referred to as an LT5/1 when the 1933 code system was introduced and it was carried by its original chassis LT345. At the time of withdrawal however it is designated as an LT3/3. (J.G.S.Smith collection)

The date is 17th August and LPTB bodied front entrance STL992, dating from April 1935, stands at Uxbridge Underground station in company with Weymann bodied T723 which first entered service in April 1946. Route 457A to Windsor Castle would be converted to RT operation with the first deliveries of this type to Windsor garage in October 1948. The single deck T was destined to be a long time resident of Uxbridge garage although here, for some reason, it is not fitted with a route blind. (J.C.Gillham)

ST1104 seen parked in the grounds of Leatherhead garage, its last Country Area home before moving to the Central Area for its last few months of passenger service. This particular bus has been shown in this series of books previously but is included here as the asymmetric lower front end is clearly shown. The era of the square cab did not last many years before the much smoother and softer rounded variety became almost universal on front engined exposed radiator passenger vehicles. (J.G.S.Smith collection)

The deserted streets and the running number AP12 both indicate it was on a Sunday that LT640 was photographed heading for Brentwood on Route 86. Although Seven Kings did gain weekday workings on this route in November only a maximum of six buses was involved on those days. The 86 was a service which had connected the East End of London with Brentwood since its introduction as 26 in February 1921. It was renumbered 86 on 1st December 1924. As with the vast majority of the class, this bus was deemed only suitable for scrap after a distinguished career which spanned from August 1931 through to July 1949. Had it not been the intervention of World War II these six wheeled AEC Renowns would almost certainly have disappeared from the streets of London long before that, being replaced by earlier delivered RTs. (J.Gascoine collection)

The classic AEC Regent 3RT chassis carried no frame extensions beyond the rear set of wheels in common with the prototype RT1. Only the 2RT2s were built with chassis member frames which continued aft of the rear wheels. On 10th May the opportunity was taken to photograph a newly delivered example standing on the brake test roadway within Chiswick Works and this picture clearly shows the layout. The fuel tank mounted on the nearside is flanked by the AEC built Wilson preselector gearbox to which belt driven dynamo and air compressor units are fitted. To the offside of the frame lies the compressed air reservoir. A larger and more efficient flywheel than that fitted to 2RT chassis is attached to the rear of the 9.6 litre engine known as the A204 variant. (L.T.Museum U39958)

This Daimler CWD6 carrying Duple bodywork was one of only thirteen delivered to London Transport and fitted when new in February 1946 with the Daimler 6 cylinder 8.25 litre engine, all the others having the AEC 7.7 litre variety. During 1950 engines from withdrawn STL class buses replaced the Daimler units. Deserted D162 lays over on Route 88 showing the five opening windows fitted which was a sure sign of movement towards peacetime standards. The 'Car Laundry' sign attached to the wall of the building in the background is curious - what a pity the enterprising owners didn't think of the term 'Car Wash' and patent it! (S.L.Poole)

Here on loan to London Transport, this Leyland LZ2 with an Alexander body seating 37 passengers first entered service in 1936 with Western SMT. Acquired by Ansell's Coaches in early 1945 via the Glasgow dealer, Sanderson, it carries the fleet name of New Karrymore Coaches Ltd. boldly on the rear panels. It was one of the earlier loans to the LPTB in 1947 and helps out on Route 12 between Dulwich Library and Oxford Circus where this photograph was taken. (J.F.Higham)

Looking rather neglected, Ransomes, Sims and Jefferies bodied ST1099 stands forlorn at Uxbridge Underground station before working a short journey to Gerrards Cross on Route 455, more normally operated by STLs. STs were unusual at High Wycombe given the hilly nature of the Buckinghamshire town and this one was a loan from Two Waters. Wisely the staff at HE have allocated it to the reasonably graded Oxford Road route. (Vanguard Bus Prints)

Red liveried ST401 on loan to Grays garage from Upton Park is photographed at Romford with an angular Massey bodied Guy having drawn up behind. At this time Grays was the extremity of London Transport bus operation, only Green Line coach 723 venturing further east to Tilbury. Bus passengers seeking the Tilbury Ferry to Gravesend would need to change to an Eastern National 37A at Grays to reach their objective. (R.Burrell)

STL212 originally entered service in September 1933 as a 3STL2, being one of a large batch of AEC petrol engined vehicles fitted with a Daimler pre-selector gearbox which first saw service from Clay Hall garage. Now fourteen years old, the bus operates from Willesden garage and is seen in Buckingham Palace Road on Route 46 as it makes its way to Alperton. (A.B.Cross)

Relieved from its previous learner duties, ST906 is pressed into service on the Epsom race course special route 406F, shuttling between Epsom Station and the Downs with racegoers. As with many ex-Tilling STs, this example went on loan during part of the war years, in this case to the Gosport and Fareham Omnibus Company who had it between December 1941 and October 1943. Built in 1930 it first entered service in October of that year and was not withdrawn from service until June 1949 to be scrapped by Daniels of Rainham. The rather bleak conditions and lack of punters suggests that the occasion was the Epsom Spring Meeting rather than the June Derby week. (J.G.S.Smith collection)

It was with a background of vehicle shortages aggravated by the non-arrival of larger numbers of the new RTs that resulted in the Board approaching the Passenger Vehicle Operators' Association for the hire of vehicles with driver for peak hour duties from October. This precarious situation was to last until 1949 when vehicle availability eased with the diversion of a number of BTC controlled Tilling Group company vehicles and other help from Maidstone and Leeds Corporations. In this photograph two antique vehicles wait at Kingston Station to spring into life in the evening peak on Route 131, while a slightly younger Bedford behind is allocated to Route 218. The lead vehicle is a Commer Invader belonging to Roberts & Dickinson who traded as Ashford Belle who also owned the second coach. The Bedford belonged to Blue and White Star Transport. (A.B.Cross)

Amersham garage had the largest concentration of the C class of buses during the latter years of operation of these small one man operated buses. Representative C42 is pictured here at Chesham having stopped to allow a passenger to alight who seems to be heading for the quaintly named "Tea Caddy" refreshment rooms. (P.Gomm collection)

Ex-Tilling STL65, still in red livery, spent much of the final eighteen months of its operational life in the Country Area garaged at Watford High Street. Here operating on the 346 route to Kingswood it clearly shows all sorts of distortion along the body length. The third ventilator above the lower deck windows has been removed and panelled over while additional sealing on the front dome helps keep out the rain. With its painted radiator surround the petrol engined bus looks totally dejected and in a sorry state compared to when it first entered service in January 1933. The picture is taken in the lower High Street passing the Monaco Motors showrooms, well known at one time for its motor racing connections and a certain racing driver by the name of Salvadori. (J.G.S.Smith collection)

This rear nearside picture of an ex-Tilling ST gives a fairly clear view of the boarding platform on an open staircase type of body, which afforded little protection from the elements to the conductor, who was expected to stand here when not collecting fares. Now in its sixteenth year, ST970 carries its second legal ownership details which on 1st January 1948 would be changed yet again with nationalisation. Used as a trainer from Cricklewood in the early part of 1947 it re-entered passenger carrying service from Seven Kings in the late summer and looks here as though it has just received a smartening up for this purpose.

The LT class was the mainstay of Leyton's Route 38 for many years and here at Victoria Station forecourt LT959 waits for its driver to move it up the narrow bay until the time comes for it to set out on its eighty eight minute journey to Chingford. A 'Bluebird' body with its square cab is carried while a diesel engine provides the motive power. Closely parked behind is a rounded cab variety with earlier built body and seating for 56 passengers as against the 60 of the front vehicle. This was accomplished by utilising a staircase built into the rear offside corner and extending the upper deck over the driver's cab. (L.T.P.S.)

Body number 11535, now mounted on the chassis of ST150, was the only example built by the Metro-Cammell Carriage and Wagon Company for the class. Twenty five similar bodies were mounted on Dennis Lance chassis in 1931 being operated by Overground Ltd. on behalf of the LGOC and eventually given fleet numbers DL1 to DL25. The ST3 body, shown here at Richmond Bus Station, first entered service on the chassis of ST211 in October 1930. It was later remounted on ST379 (9/31), ST589 (10/32), ST478 (10/33), ST359 (10/34) finally reaching ST150 in November 1935 where it was to stay until withdrawn from service in May 1948 being scrapped the following month. The all metal body was easily distinguishable by its flat lower panelling devoid of the usual mouldings, square corners to the window frames and different profile to the roof. (V.C.Jones)

The railway bridge at Worcester Park Station prevented normal height double deck buses using this link between North Cheam and Malden until the road was lowered in 1963. Only single deck vehicles on Route 213 or lowbridge double deckers on Route 127 were using this road, the A2043, in the year under review. LT1060 carrying an LTL1/1 body, which type was fitted with a rear blind box, easily passes under the restricted clearance as it makes its way to Kingston. A dealer in Newport in South Wales by the name of Morgan took thirty six of these withdrawn single.deck LTs from London Transport in the early 50s, this bus being one of them. At least three were exported to Yugoslavia, which begs the question were there more and did this one go there? (Omnibus Society)

Two Waters garage provided the first accommodation for T658 upon its return to peacetime duties. From his shelter under the shop blind in St.Albans Road, the photographer captures a shot of the coach in Watford working the horseshoe shaped 318 route from Abbots Langley to Bucks Hill, hotly pursued by an ST on Route 334A heading for Watford (Met) Station. The stepped type of blind display was favoured by the Country Area for its more convoluted routes. (P.Gomm collection)

The original Green Line route 725 between Chesham, Amersham and Oxford Circus began operation on 19th June 1946 only to be withdrawn on 12th November of the following year being replaced by the extension of the Godstone route 709 to Chesham and the Crawley route 710 to Amersham. Q222c, an Amersham based coach, makes its way across Ealing Common in August en route to Amersham on the half hourly service, every other coach continuing into Chesham providing that town with an hourly service. A police box stands across the road, later to provide inspiration to the writers of Doctor Who, while the overhead wiring is for trolleybus routes 607 and 655. (L.T.Museum U40687)

If you had chipped away at the paintwork of D69 when its body was removed by Harkness of Belfast in 1955 prior to receiving a new one, you might have revealed several layers demonstrating its chequered career. Initially entering service in May 1945 in grey it was repainted red in February of the year under review. In 1948 the Romford Green Line double deck routes needed augmenting and it was one of five Central Area Ds repainted green for this purpose. Made redundant by new RTs in the summer of 1950 it returned to Merton garage and red livery. On top of this it may have received a coat of Belfast paint after arriving there in 1954. Here it passes along Whitehall in its recently acquired red livery passing a pre-war Austin taxi as it makes its way to Clapham Common on Route 88. (S.A.Newman)

On the night of 17th/18th March eleven different special routes were introduced to transport MPs home from the Houses of Parliament if the House rose after 11.45p.m. On that first night the sitting ended at 1.22a.m. but fewer than a dozen MPs plus some officials and journalists travelled on the buses. Here various vehicles wait patiently in the small hours. At the front from right to left are LT169, STL2306 and STL679. A Q class bus and at least one further STL can be seen in the far distance. Due to lack of usage the buses only ran if specially requested after Parliament returned from the Whitsun recess on 3rd June. Note the slipboards carried beneath the canopies indicating the special route numbers on which the buses are operating.

Catford's STL1982 makes its way to Welling over Shooters Hill on Route 89. This batch of STLs carried rather odd registrations and this vehicle was one of only three to carry BYY index letters. Somewhere along the line its body has lost its roofbox and the radiator surround has gained a dull black coat. The 'modern' concrete roadway, which gave an irritating "bomp bomp" effect when driving at speed, shows up well in this picture as does the very long exposure speed used by the photographer, emphasised by the pedestrian's legs. (K.A.V.Newley collection)

ST82, seen parked at Epping Garage, had an eventful career in its latter years with London Transport, having first entered service form Hanwell garage in March 1930 in red livery. Converted to operate with producer gas trailer from August 1942 until November 1944, it was repainted into Country Area livery just before this episode ended. Wearing its later livery with painted radiator shell and now carrying LGOC body number 11521 of type ST1/1, it is ready to leave on Route 392 to Ongar. This route originated when the pre-war Green Line service to Ongar was withdrawn and was to disappear on 12th November, being absorbed into 339 which prior to this had operated remotely between Ongar or Coxtie Green and Warley. (R.Burrell)

ST914 is pressed back into service from its more usual duties as a staff bus or trainer which have occupied its time since return from temporary exile in the provinces. From December 1941 to March 1944 it was loaned to the Trent Motor Traction Company. An enterprising employee of LPTB has very precisely applied route bills of the type used on the hired coaches to the front for the ex-Tilling's temporary use on Route 14. In addition a proper roller blind has also been acquired from somewhere. The familiar background of Oxford Road at Putney provides the stand for this rather antiquated seventeen year old. (J.G.S.Smith collection)

Having brought a private party to the race course on 7th June, former Daimler DST5, registered GO5538 rests on the grassy parking area with other contemporaries. Originally a double deck bus operated in London by Redline (E.Brickwood) with Birch bodywork for 52 passengers it was rebodied with this Park Royal coach type with 31 seats and operated by Roberts of Connahs Quay, first of many owners, after the chassis had been disposed of by LPTB in 1936. The body was used for mounting on a new and shortened STL chassis which entered service in October 1936 as STL1262. In 1947 when this picture was taken the coach is recorded as being owned by Brown of Brimington near Chesterfield. (A.B.Cross)

One of the ex-Tilling STLs exiled into Hertfordshire in December 1946 and now wearing unfamiliar green, STL115 was destined to return home to Bromley for a spell before its final demise in September 1949. Here it accelerates gently away from traffic lights, with a tail of vehicles typical of the 1947 scene, en-route to the delightfully countrified name of 'Harebreaks' on Route 345. This illusion of rural England was unfortunately quickly dispelled when you arrived in this north Watford suburb and the bus reversed into Leggatts Way by the Harebreaks Recreation Ground. (J.G.S.Smith collection)

RT163 entered service in August, being garaged at Leyton and helping to replace open staircase LTs, many of which passed on for use at other garages although the original intention had been to dispose of them. The bus is pausing outside the Royal Forest Hotel en-route from High Beach to Clapham Common on Route 35A although the pillar route stencil displays the bare 35 number from which route most of the Saturday allocation was derived. As to the advertisement on the side, I prefer brown coffee but this was obviously a misguided attempt at patriotism! (S.L.Poole)

LT1248 received a renovation at the hands of the workforce of Mann Egerton during October and November 1946. It stands here on the Old Maypole terminus lay-by at the junction of New North Road and Fencepiece Road in Barkingside before journeying to Ilford Station on Route 25A. This site, now built on, was at one time the location of a proposed new garage which never materialised. The 'Bluebird' LT with its LT6/4 type body, number 13233, was withdrawn from service to depart for Daniels scrapyard at Rainham in August 1949. (R.Burrell)

The front wheel trim of C111 is now painted although the general appearance of the vehicle suggests further attention is now overdue. Seen standing beside Victoria garage, with a British Airways board hiding its Inter Station transfers, it carries its customary Old Kent Road stencil. During their service with London Transport these Cs were always garaged at P until transferred en bloc to GM for other uses during the early part of 1951, eventually being totally withdrawn from service in October 1951. The London Fire Brigade in due course acquired this vehicle putting it to work as a control unit and it now enjoys preserved status.

A small number of vehicles were acquired from independents by London Transport in 1933 and numbered in the STL class, being given numbers 553 to 558. STL557, the highest numbered from the fleet of C.H.Pickup of SW9 is depicted here at Shoreditch Church in the final full year of its operation, being withdrawn from service in July 1948 to be reduced to scrap. It had been licensed for service on 1st July 1932 having an open top body as favoured by Pickup built by Park Royal. Wooden seating was provided on the upper deck for 30 passengers while the lower saloon held 26 on moquette covered seating. It was in May 1934 that STL557 became the first of the five to receive a complete Chiswick built top deck which did not match the Park Royal constructed lower portion. It was in this guise that it continued in service classified as a 1/12STL8.

Service vehicle 39H has a long history stretching back to 1928 when as NS2295 it first entered service from Cricklewood garage. The chassis, an AEC Model 4, is married to an LGOC built body which originally seated 51 passengers. It ended its passenger service career in London during 1937, by then fitted with pneumatic tyres, covered top and driver's windscreen, all of which were lacking when the first of the type entered service in 1923. In its final form it is viewed at Chelsham garage in October in use as a 7 ton mobile staff canteen, one of twelve NS type buses so converted during 1936/7. It was the second to last of the batch to be disposed of in April 1951. (J.W.Millbank)

Just a few days after entering service at Croydon garage in August RT154 is seen at the Croydon Airport terminus of Route 115. A few passengers have availed themselves of the superior conditions offered by this Park Royal bodied bus while those wishing to travel on the Route 194 service are offered LT539, an Elmers End bus, more typical of transport for this period. The body of the RT, number 1403, had been placed on another chassis by the time the vehicle was disposed of in March 1958. At that time RT154 carried a Weymann body number 5950 originally mounted on the chassis of RT3069, a 1951 delivery. Bradford City Transport then operated the bus as their fleet number 401 through to May 1969 when it went to Autospares Ltd. of Bingley. (J.W.Millbank)

When it was realised that delivery of chassis would outstrip the building capacity of Weymann and Park Royal additional bodybuilders were sought by London Transport. In the end Saunders Engineering and Shipyard Ltd. of Beaumaris and Cravens Railway Carriage and Wagon Co. Ltd. of Sheffield were given orders. In August 1947 RT410 was sent to both Saunders and Cravens to enable the new builders to examine a standard RT body. The bus is seen here at the Isle of Anglesey premises of Saunders in August with craftsmen noting details of the Weymann produced body prior to commencing building their initial contract for 250 bodies. Interestingly while Cravens produced what was basically their standard body cosmetically altered to meet London requirements, Saunders decided in the end to mimic the RT3 body as far as possible. (Courtesy of Saunders' Archives)

This picture shows well the comparison in the early 1930s between the design styles of Thomas Tilling and the LGOC. ST925 represents Tilling and LT847 the LGOC. The antiquated style of the Tilling STs and their generally down at heel appearance by 1947 definitely made them second best. Both buses are working Route 21 from Old Kent Road garage and are captured on film at Finsbury Square, Moorgate, the northern terminus of the route since it was cut back from Turnpike Lane in 1942. (A.B.Cross)

Older film buffs might remember the film 'Time Out of Mind' but to London Transport enthusiasts it is purely another different advertisement seen on buses of the era. ST27 operates from Hammersmith garage while employed on Route 49 with the blind set for a journey to Streatham Common. This was more usual for this garage's allocation rather than the full extent of the journey to Crystal Palace. Hammersmith's association with this route began in 1943 when they replaced Turnham Green but on 12th November of the year under review they were themselves replaced by Battersea garage who contributed STLs to the route.

Having just disgorged its passengers in the High Street at Epsom, ST1124b momentarily stands in front of an ornamental awning to a tobacconists which is still decorated with blackout paint work. The driver's attention seems to be drawn by something - could it be the lady with sunglasses lurking beneath the awning? The summer dresses of the pedestrians and the open necked shirt and braces worn by the driver suggest it is a pleasant July day for those venturing out, especially on Route 468 which operated between the town and Chessington Zoo. (D.W.K.Jones)

This array of vehicles was caught on film on Monday 6th October 1947 at Old Town, Clapham Common. From left to right we have RT184, STL412, STL904, STL1775, RT177 and an STL on Route 5A whose identification is defeated by the inadequacies of the camera lens. The Leyton drivers on Route 35 were no doubt very proud of the way their gleaming new charges stood out in such company. (A.B.Cross)

ST694's body had been strengthened by Mann Egerton during August and September 1946, which must have helped its longevity, since it was one of the last standard STs to be withdrawn from service in January 1950. It is seen standing in St.Andrews Road, Romford behind the former Hillman's garage, by now known as Romford, London Road Green Line garage. Route blinds carried show the bus to be in use on a short eastern section of Route 86 while operating from Seven Kings garage. The body carried is number 12343, first fitted to ST717 and the bus ended its career with London Transport classified as a 1ST2. (R.Burrell)

The route number 133 was a product of the 1924 renumbering scheme when it, together with a 134 route, grew out of the old 34 route and its variations. Although running between Liverpool Street and West Wickham on weekdays from 1924 to October 1927, the present 133 has evolved from a route started on 27th March 1929 between Liverpool Street and South Croydon which was a diversion and renumbering of 34 and was initially worked by Streatham and Hackney garages. Croydon garage became involved in the route's operation in 1938 and here their STL52 awaits departure on the old terminal stand in Liverpool Street from which the route was evicted on 23rd July of the year under review. Thereafter the route worked from Finsbury Circus until restored to a closer proximity to Liverpool Street Station when the new bus station opened in May 1992. (G.F.Ashwell)

Under the scheme whereby London Transport hired coaches and drivers to assist in vehicle deficiencies, there were some which were used on Country Area services. Bookham Saloons supplied this AEC Regal with registration BKT602. Here it stands awaiting departure on Route 406 from the relatively new facilities at Kingston Station together with an ST and an STL. (A.B.Cross)

LT913 finished its public service career with London Transport as a 12LT5/5 carrying body number 12831, of which just over one hundred examples (numbered 12798 to 12901) were produced. Earlier double deckers with route boards had always provided a three piece display but these LTs were the first to feature the three piece roller blinds which were to remain the standard for double deck buses in London until comparatively recent times. Although full use of these blinds had been made in pre-war times, full utilisation did not return to London until 1950 and never on a vehicle of this age. This scene with the long shadows of a sunny winter's afternoon is at Muswell Hill Broadway. (C.Carter)

While working duty TB33 on Route 47 from Bromley garage STL175 passes through the City on its way south. In later life the chassis was used to build service vehicle 739J and in this form it has been shown in previously published volumes in this series. Here in its original form its external appearance matches the one hundred vehicles numbered STL1 - 50 and 153 - 202 which entered service in 1933 although mechanically there were two distinctly different variations within the batch which London Transport coded accordingly 1STL and 2STL. (J.G.S.Smith collection)

"Now look, this is Tattenham Corner, you're supposed to be running round here with me on your back you stupid horse." Just why this conversation appears to be taking place is uncertain but what is for sure is that a Country Area ST with square cab, identifying it as a former East Surrey vehicle, has been used on a private hire assignment to the famous Epsom racecourse on 5th June. The purpose of the picture was obviously to illustrate the prominent advertisement on the side of the bus but perhaps the photographer also had some monetary interest in the aforementioned quadruped. (Courtesy of Whitbread Archives)

Lowbridge ST157b with its body built by Short Bros. of Rochester is seen at Watford on Route 336 at the beginning of its journey to Chesham, Nashleigh Arms. The oval shaped window is still in place but it would lose this on its next visit to Chiswick Works for overhaul. The advertisement on the hoarding is intriguing, reading 'Go easy in the danger hours. Use your current by the clock to safeguard Britain's recovery programme'. 8.00a.m. to 10.00a.m. and 4.00p.m. to 5.30p.m. are identified as the peak demand periods for electricity. A Vauxhall 14 car follows behind the ST the JK registration of which was current right through from 1928 to February 1948. (L.T.P.S.)

Piccadilly is remarkably quiet in this scene on Saturday 28th June in which STD160, one of the initial batch to enter service from Loughton garage in November 1946, makes its way to Victoria on Route 38A. The two front advertisements are for the London Music Festival which is now in full swing at the Harringay Arena from June 7th through to July 6th. It must have made a nice change from the ice hockey and speedway, not to mention the doggies. (G.F.Ashwell)

Heinz quality foods are still with us while the Fifty Shilling Tailors now trade under a new name and image. The facade of Tooting Broadway still looks much the same as here although the temporary lack of full glazing to the shop front is just a memory as too is D209 setting out on Route 80 to Lower Kingswood. This bus had only entered service in July of the previous year, being one of a hundred of the class purchased to help relieve the need for new vehicles immediately after the war. The bus was to end its days in totally different surroundings in Ceylon. (W.J.Haynes)

Most photographers rushed to Victoria to take the new RTs on Route 10 but on Sunday the route terminated at Elephant & Castle which is where this picture of RT152 was taken in June. London Passenger Transport Board are shown as the legal owners but less than 200 of these vehicles carried this name since from 1st January 1948 it would be changed to the new London Transport Executive. The conductor with Bell Punch ticket equipment stands on the rear platform seemingly well trained in the official pose. (G.F.Ashwell)

Resting from its duties on the Inter-Station service following the route curiously displayed on the blind placed in the recessed window by the passenger saloon door, C107 is now returned to its normal colour scheme of blue and cream. All eight of these unusual deck and a half coaches, with seating for 20 passengers and plenty of luggage space beneath the raised rear portion, were chiefly used on the Inter-Station service from the second half of 1936. During the war several were repainted khaki for loan to ENSA for the conveyance of entertainers for the forces. It was not until 1947 that they fully resumed responsibility for the Inter-Station service releasing the last two blue and cream liveried STs which had been adapted for the role. In 1950 they were replaced by conventional RT type buses but they did see one more short spell of passenger use, being hired to British European Airways in 1951 before their final withdrawal and disposal. (Lens of Sutton)

Having only recently received an overhaul and now looking refreshed, RT147 will soon be returned to Putney Bridge garage from its temporary photographic venture within Chiswick Works on 15th June. Most unfortunate though is the absence of the wheel trims with which the bus would have first entered service in March 1941 and the painting over of the roof mounted roof box which, though admittedly not of great practicality, gave these buses when new a quirky identity all their own. (L.T.Museum U40225)

LT1092 was another bus to retain its perimeter seating right through to the end of its operational life which occurred in March 1949, having been converted in February 1942. The conversion reduced seating from 35 passengers to 33 but allowed space for twenty standing passengers, a much needed life line for additional operating capacity at this period in the history of London Transport. The residential properties appear to have come through the war years unscathed while a solitary standing gas light will provide minimal illumination in the hours of darkness. This view is typical of the 236 route which originated as 263 and followed secondary roads used by independent bus operators to avoid the restricted streets imposed by the 1924 London Traffic Act. (C.Carter)

Wearing the relatively short lived first post-war colour scheme, STL1249 carries an unusual registration not dissimilar to the later 'cherished' series used on Routemasters. In passing STL1981 also carried a plate CLT303, these being the only two instances where the base letters LT were used on STL vehicles. The body of this bus, number 15727, had been fitted to this chassis since July 1939 and STL1249 had always been fitted with an STL11 body through all its various visits to Chiswick. The bus here is parked alongside its home Streatham garage. (A.B.Cross)

This view of Purley High Street appears to have been taken from the top deck of a tram on Service 16/18 as it waited to depart for the Embankment. STL42 approaches on its way to Old Coulsdon on the Sunday only section of Route 159 from Thornton Heath. It is recorded that after withdrawal in April 1948 the body of this STL was burnt the following month while the chassis was used as the basis for service vehicle 741J.

This is TF77 which now forms part of the London Transport Museum collection and can be seen currently at Covent Garden. It was transferred to the collection in April 1954 but some years earlier it is viewed standing at Dorking Bus Station working Route 713 through to Dunstable. The entire production batch of TFs were delivered during 1939 and interestingly LPTB began a new series of body numbers with this class, TF2 - 88 being numbered 1 to 87. The previous series, which had been in continual use since the system had been introduced, had reached 18365, which was the number given to one of the three spare T10/1 type bodies built. (R.Wellings collection)

This particular view of RT152, standing at the Elephant & Castle in the newest red and cream livery with black mudguards and shining radiator shell and wheel trims, also shows the plain body panel aft of the rearmost lower saloon window. Before completion of the earliest RT3 bodies it had been decided to fit an offside route number plate but with the non-availability of the bracket in quantity at the body builders, the incorporation of this fitment had to wait until 1948 after the first 114 vehicles had already been built. (G.F.Ashwell)

This 2/1ST9 originally operated with the National Omnibus and Transport Co.Ltd. on behalf of the LGOC when it first entered service in April 1930. In this view ST129, still with the smaller route blind box with which it was built, operates as HG13 on Route 310 and is seen at Waltham Cross. Since the formation of LPTB the bus has worn Country Area colours. (R.Burrell)

Another CR bus which was put to good use by Merton garage was CR6 which, together with the earlier example shown in use on the same route, had managed to enter service at Kingston garage in the month war was declared. Because of their then revolutionary design with a rear mounted engine, only 49 were built by Leyland Motors in close working collaboration with the LPTB and spares soon became a problem. They were ultimately put into store for the duration of hostilities. Fitment of an offside route number bracket was to fall out of favour with the result that no further single deckers were ever fitted with this anachronism. The class reappeared from storage in 1946 but were mainly used as relief vehicles in the Central Area.

Route number 150 had lain dormant since 9th October 1938 until resurrected on 26th February for a new daily route to serve the expanding Hainault estate. Leyton garage provided two T class buses for the service, which operated between the 'Old Maypole' at Barkingside and Regarder Road on Manford Way, although at weekends an LT bus was sometimes substituted from its normal usage on Route 236. LT1129 is seen on the purpose built stand at Barkingside. The use of a route number below 200 for a single deck route was unique at the time but since work was underway on altering the headroom under the railway bridge in New North Road which necessitated the single deckers, it was probably done to avoid a renumbering after December 10th when the route was converted to double deck and extended to Chigwell Row. In the 1950 book of this series this particular bus can be seen after its rebuild by Marshalls of Cambridge. (R.Burrell)

STL1793 is seen on 26th April just five months before it lost its centre entrance body (number 17722) which had been used in the 'Pay As You Board' experiments. It was replaced by a standard rear entrance example numbered 17079 which can be seen on page 93 of the 1950 book in this series. The bus had been transferred to the Country Area in August 1945 still wearing its Central Area livery and is seen here in use from Reigate garage with a normal roving conductor. For an offside view of this unique body the reader is referred to the supplement section at page 111 of the 1946 book. (L.Housden collection)

Alongside the patched up brickwork of Chiltern Court and Baker Street Station after the wartime bomb, Green Line D161 is showing the least informative type of private blind. In later years the operator's name and address would be added to such displays although the "I'm sorry" syndrome was a long way off! Originally when delivered the cab window surround was painted green but having gained a repaint into two-tone green livery the complete window surround is now finished in the lighter colour. The bus is presumably awaiting duty on the 726 to Whipsnade Zoo. (S.A.Newman)

The lifelong fitment of an STL3 body to one chassis was unusual but not unique. STL350, having been outshopped from overhaul at Chiswick in July with body number 13704 would continue in daily use until May 1950 having first entered service in February 1934. Except for variations in the paint scheme, a change of fleet name and legal ownership details, little else has changed since its initial entry into service from Hanwell garage on Route 55 some thirteen and a half years earlier. Minor differences include a route number stencil holder above the rearmost lower saloon window, loss of the kerbside guide stalk, masking of the blind apertures and the addition of a nearside driver's mirror. Only the first twenty five bodies of the basic STL3 design incorporated a ventilator in the front dome and the chassis was fitted with an oil engine and preselector gearbox with fluid flywheel from new. This photo was taken at Chiswick to show the commercial advertising spaces. While the Route 88 blinds fitted were appropriate for its subsequent allocation to Merton, the Putney Bridge garage plate was presumably the only one the Chiswick staff could lay their hands on at the time. (L.T.Museum U40487)

Wearing the brown and cream livery in which it had first entered service in August 1945 NCME bodied G235 would eventually lose its non standard colours in January 1949. Its initial home was Victoria garage but the entire stock of Guys allocated to this garage was transferred en-bloc to Enfield in November 1945 and there it stayed until along with sister G236 it found a new home at Upton Park. In service until November 1952 it was acquired by Western SMT in March 1953 and operated as their fleet number 1028 for several years. Here it stands alongside Enfield garage while being used on the short 121 route to Chingford. Through many changes the only section of the route as it was in 1947 which remains today is the couple of hundred yards between the garage and Hertford Road. (A.B.Cross)

Nearing the end of its journey from Stoke Newington on Route 67, ST864 is about to cross the River Thames by way of Waterloo Bridge. The badly wound blinds may reflect the inadequacies of the aged mechanism or possibly just a lazy conductor, although in 1947 that is unlikely. Tottenham garage had received this ex-Tilling open staircase bus from Cricklewood garage on 8th August, holding on to it until 15th October when it was returned. On 24th June 1948 it was dispatched to Chiswick Works and promptly withdrawn. Norwood garage, who by then had operated it for around six weeks probably thought this was the best outcome for the eighteen year old. (V.C.Jones)

Rather surprisingly six former Tilling STLs were repainted green during 1947 and 1948, having always previously been in red livery and allocated to ex-Tilling garages. These six vehicles plus others of the type at various times were to become a common sight during the period usually on peak hour services operated by Watford High Street and Two Waters garages. STL117, the first to receive the new livery in August 1947, is seen operating on Route 301B in Woodford Road at Watford Junction. No attempt was made to apply a 'modern' livery to these buses and standard green and off white was used. (J.G.S.Smith collection)

During 1947 red ST778 is recorded as being allocated to Upton Park garage. Here however it is seen at Sevenoaks Bus Station working for Northfleet garage on the 401 route, which was normally operated from either Dunton Green, Swanley Junction or Dartford. It is also equipped with a very unusual blind. These blinds were ordered for use at Easter 1947 and carried just six single line destinations for Route 401. They were also used at Easter the following year but it is not certain what event it was that called for the extra vehicles and special blinds, although Brands Hatch does spring to mind as a possibility. A contemporary Maidstone & District bus stands alongside while a 10T10 Green Line coach edges into the picture on the left. (J.G.S.Smith collection)

Venture Transport (Hendon) Ltd. loaned this AEC Regal coach to London Transport in 1947 which was put to work on Route 16. Held in Park Lane at a pedestrian crossing before the days of zebra stripes it operates on the service between Victoria and Neasden, not 'Venturing' (sorry!!) as far as Sudbury Town. (P.J.Marshall)

LT547 managed to complete over eighteen years service with London Transport before being withdrawn and disposed of in January 1950, the last month of operation of the double deck element of the class. This no doubt had been partly achieved by the renovation it received at the hands of Mann Egerton, Norwich in February 1946 and again with more thorough treatment by Marshalls of Cambridge in December of the same year which took two months to complete. This double treatment was a phenomenon which often happened within the class. Certainly the wood framed body shows no sign of sag and the bus looks in reasonable condition except for the battered front offside mudguard. It is seen at Charing Cross on Route 11 while working from Dalston garage. (J.G.S.Smith collection)

A varied range of vehicles occupy the interior of Victoria garage on 18th February with the unique TF9 easily recognisable in the middle distance. From the left hand side and working in a clockwise direction, two STLs with different colour schemes stand behind a 7T7 class bus with an STL and post war STD in front. In the far distance with most vehicles standing over the pits, a solitary LT together with five STLs can be seen. Among the array of vehicles a service lorry is just visible before five more STLs are encountered. One of these is in the short lived all red with two cream bands livery and finally a solitary wartime STD is seen with two further STLs completing the picture. The one nearest the camera is STL1140. The 7T7 and the LT are obvious interlopers and the LT is interesting in that the larger rear blind box appears to be in use instead of the more usual single line blind. (L.T.Museum 20697)

Something of a mixture is revealed in this view of a trio of G class vehicles parked at Hornchurch garage. Nearest the camera G258 is fitted with a Massey body finished in a livery of two shades of brown, while G247 the middle vehicle is an NCME bodied variety. The furthest from the camera, G204, carries a Park Royal body and all three show garage journeys for the routes they were previously employed on, either 175 or 123. It is interesting to note the three different body builders' approach to the bottom finish of the driver's windscreen with a surprisingly nice curvature to the Massey example, which was in fact the most angular of the designs. (J.Lines collection)

The highest numbered AEC Renown six wheeled double deck was LT1426 delivered in November 1932 to the LGOC. In 1932 when diesel engines were the subject of much experimentation it was decided to fit Gardner diesel units to the batch LT1417 through to LT1426 from new. As these engines were longer than their AEC counterparts they required the radiator being moved forward which produced a recognisable snout. To compensate for the extended forward length the saloon body was reduced by $3\frac{1}{2}$" which was accomplished by reducing the length at the rear resulting in a narrower boarding platform and slightly reduced length rear saloon windows to the upper deck. This enabled the length of the bus to be kept within the maximum permitted by the regulations. Two ventilator louvres were fitted side by side beneath the driver's windscreen which were deemed necessary due to the lack of a cooling fan. Their uniqueness ensured that these bodies were retained on the original chassis all through their working lives with London Transport although the majority later received AEC engines. LT1426 stands at the Wanstead terminus of the frequent Route 101. (R.Burrell)

G321 a Park Royal bodied Guy Arab II crosses the bascule bridge on Woolwich Manor Way which at times played havoc with the schedules on Route 101. This was the bridge which suffered damage from a V2 rocket on 22nd February 1945 and remained closed to traffic until 6th July 1947 necessitating a long diversion through the docks themselves. The driver gives the cyclists a wide berth which he can afford to do in the traffic free conditions. The "See you at Butlins this summer" advertisement shows the comparatively short time it took to return to peacetime pursuits. Still carrying its red and broken white livery the bus operates from Upton Park garage where it had first entered service eighteen months earlier. (Docklands Museum)

Ex-NS521 now lovingly named 'Majole' - the meaning of which escapes us - now resides behind a trellis fencing to be partly hidden when the climbing rose next awakes into life. The four wooden blocks which would have supported the route boards are still firmly in place while the central glazed portion above would have been mostly obscured with the route number stencil. (N.Rayfield)

These two pages are included unashamedly to give younger readers an idea of the many treasures which could be found by dint of exploration in the 1940s. This photograph was taken on 8th August and what was once NS109 rests alongside the hedgerow having not received as much attention as some other NSs residing in this corner of Hayling Island. This picture does give a perfect view of the solid wheels still fitted to all the buses on these two pages. All four had entered service in 1923 being sold for further use during 1934 through C & P Sales of Balham. (G.F.Ashwell)

Oh to turn back the clock to those exciting seaside holidays on Hayling Island in the early post-war era! A magnificent sight awaited anyone who rode the 'Puffing Billy' rail service from Havant and negotiated the narrow lanes to the more remote early establishments which were the beginnings of the caravan and leisure park of today's holiday scene. Above, ex-NS480, nicely revamped to provide comfortable accommodation, looks majestic in its final years as it sits among the summer flowers within its own little plot of land. While below what was once NS768 clearly shows the 'General' name embellished at the top of its radiator and still has its fleet number plate attached to the side of the bonnet. Another bus body behind has been used as the core of a construction but the ventilators suggest this was not of LGOC origin. (Both photos N.Rayfield)

Service vehicles are not normally included within the pages of this series of books unless they started life as a bus or coach. But there are exceptions and this view of a 6 ton tower wagon, with operators working on the wires in Clarence Street, Kingston, having originally entered service in July 1930 had to be included. With bomb damage and the elongated notice exhorting one to keep on saving as a background to the ADC model 418 chassis with fleet number 8E the scene of the period justified inclusion. (John McMillen)

G150 carried the only Park Royal built body of all metal construction delivered to London Transport during the 'austerity' period. Other bodies of similar construction were supplied, notably by NCME, but as to the reason why Park Royal supplied just this one body from a total of 211 can only be construed as preparation for peacetime production methods. Refinements fitted included windows set in pans, five sliding type vents to each side and a more rounded roof dome. It resided at Alperton garage from the time of its entry into service in September 1945 until July 1952. Disposed of to North's it was eventually acquired by W.S.Rowbotham of Harriseahead. This business was taken over by the Potteries Motor Traction Co.Ltd. in January 1959 and fleet number H470 was carried during its short life with this operator before disposal to F.Cowley, a Salford dealer, in November 1960. Here it is displaying a blind for the Sunday working on Route 72 from Esher to North Wembley. (J.C.Gillham)

G101 with Park Royal manufactured bodywork heads along the Kingston By Pass on its journey to Chessington Zoo on Route 72A. This was a summer weekend service which ran each year from 1946 to 1950 following the 72 route from North Wembley or East Acton in 1949 and 1950 turning off at Hook to take people like those at the front upstairs on this bus to see the animals. In the right background a line of pre-fab type dwellings can be seen while to the left of the picture a Singer Bantam car of the period 1935-1939 passes the bus at speed (relatively speaking of course!). An American Ford Lincoln is parked close to the kerb behind. (A.B.Cross)

T414b returned to bus duties after the war as was the case with the forty nine still owned from the original T403 to T452 batch of 9T9. Most were used in the Country Area but a few could be seen on Central Area duties. When built in 1936 they represented the first series of new Green Line coaches to be introduced by LPTB and enabled the first large scale clear out of a number of coaches of various makes and sizes which had been acquired from independent operators in 1933/34. Here at Staines this fine looking Weymann bodied AEC Regal rests from duties on route 462 before returning to Leatherhead while further along the road an LGOC bodied AEC Regent of the ST class will soon be departing for the Red Lion at Thorpe. (M.Rooum)

Originally fitted with a Gardner 6LW engine, LT1422 first appeared on the streets of London in November 1932 operating from Hanwell garage where the Gardner engined batch were to remain until driver resistance to these 9LT7 coded vehicles caused them to be moved. LT1422 arrived at Leyton early in 1947. All but two from the batch LT1417 to LT1426 were changed to using AEC 8.8 litre engines, the two which were not so converted being LT1420 and LT1424. This change of engine so late in their lives did not extend their operational life and all of the batch had been withdrawn from use by the end of 1949. (J.G.S.Smith collection)

The unmistakable iron and glass roof of Victoria Station looms over well laden T483c as it pauses on Eccleston Bridge on its long journey from Hemel Hempstead to East Grinstead. The coach carries EG garage plates although it is actually one of Two Waters' vehicles, its home since returning to Green Line duties after the war. The coach driver and an inspector converse with each other, probably about the running of the vehicle or timings to be met. (W.J.Haynes)

Although Kingston in pre-war days had a small allocation of 5Q5s, used mainly on Route 201, these were removed in March 1940. However in post-war years they frequently borrowed such vehicles from elsewhere to help out - more usually on Route 213. Here however Dalston based Q110 has travelled to the south-west and is employed on Route 216 to Staines. (D.A.Ruddom collection)

Obviously the LGOC considered adequate ventilation was provided with their body design without recourse to roof ducts if one compares this similar view with the ex-Tilling STL shown earlier in this volume. The vehicle details are not known but nevertheless an unusual view of an LT class bus operated by Elmers End garage on Route 12 is afforded the reader. Unaware of the photographer above, a man on the bus platform finds an excuse to give the lady a helping hand while another man uses the tramway section feeder pillar to support himself while tying his shoelace. (L.Housden collection)

Staines via Sunbury is the destination carried by T314 as it stands in the Kingston railway station terminus sometime in August waiting its turn to take up duties on Route 216. This bus had first entered service in October 1932 being owned by the LGOC but operated by Thomas Tilling Ltd. in their distinctive livery. Cosmetic differences besides its livery change include the loss of one opening window; the reduction of the blind box to standard LT width, although the height defied standardisation and the moving of the sidelights from suspension beneath the driver's canopy to the more acceptable position. Otherwise the bus has faithfully kept its distinctive Tilling profile. (V.C.Jones)

A fairly substantial number of ex-T and C class vehicles were exported to war ravaged mainland Europe in 1945. The Ts to the War Department for Control Commission, Germany and the Cs to the Belgian Economic Mission. One of the ex-1/7T7/1 Green Line 30 seat coaches, which mainly entered service in 1931, is photographed in Douai, France suitably rebuilt with a front entrance on the driver's side. This vehicle was once T263 and first saw service from Tunbridge Wells. The Weymann built body was fitted with a standard LPTB one piece route box in July 1938 when its Green Line duties ceased, seating being altered to longitudinal layout in 1942. It now carries the fleet name 'Autocars, Douaisiens' and French registration number 1387MD9. (J.H.Price)

STL187 has been shown before in this series of books. This time it is viewed in use from Croydon garage on Route 64 as it journeys to Selsdon, Being one of twenty five with STL1 type bodies ordered by the outgoing LGOC and still under construction at the formation of LPTB on 1st July 1933 it was to enter service at Elmers End on the 14th of that month. The body had been given number 13576 continuing a series started by the LGOC at its very beginnings. The chassis and body code, in this instance 2STL1, was a new system introduced in March 1934. The codes were applied throughout the fleet upon vehicles receiving overhauls at Chiswick and was extended to new deliveries from May 1934 onwards. (R.F.Mack)

Two Waters garage at Hemel Hempstead was opened in 1935 as part of a major building programme undertaken in the 1934 to 1936 period to provide well placed bus and coach bases for the Country Area. During this time Epping was opened in 1934 followed by Grays, Hertford and Two Waters finishing with St.Albans and Northfleet in 1936 together with the newer Amersham building. This interior view of the pit area within HH on 26th March shows the use of natural lighting as far as possible together with an assortment of vehicles. From left to right are a 4Q4 with its blinds showing "School Special"; Q85; ST592; Q95; ST302 and T656. ST592 had been repainted into Country Area livery in September 1944 while ST302 had received similar treatment in August 1946. The other vehicles had all been delivered in green colours although Q85 would receive post-war all over red in 1948 and be transferred to the Central Area, initially for operation from Dalston garage on Route 208. (L.T.Museum U39394)

— 1948 —

Weekend rail replacement services are nothing new and on Sunday 11th April 1948 track relaying meant that buses replaced trains between Wimbledon and Clapham Junction. D17 stands on the forecourt of Wimbledon Station, being part of nearby Merton garage's contribution to the relief operation. (V.C.Jones)

On 5th June 1948 at Epsom Town Station Green Line liveried STL2637, normally resident at Romford, London Road garage but now carrying RG garage plates, helps out in moving those interested in reaching the local racecourse. This combination of AEC Regent chassis number 06616738 and LPTB built body of STL16 style number 214, were to go their separate ways in the following year. The chassis provided the basis for SRT61 which went into service in June, while the body found an immediate new foundation mounted on the chassis of STL2140 replacing a metal framed Park Royal body suffering from corrosion. (A.B.Cross)

Left and opposite top.

It would appear from these photographs that Dean and Dawson have hired some London Transport vehicles – could it be as many as 31 I wonder? – to transport the members of some organisation to Westminster. Taken on Saturday 24th April 1948, ST861 is seen passing the familiar stripey buildings of New Scotland Yard on Victoria Embankment.

Saturday, 5th June 1948 and a large number of antiquated London Transport vehicles have assembled on Epsom Downs to move the punters between the racecourse and Morden Station. LT85 nearest the camera is temporarily deserted by its crew while the driver of LT13 still sits in his cab as his conductor surveys the scene in conversation with a gentleman on crutches. The lower numbered of the LTs was taken out of service in September of this year while the other example lasted a little while longer, its service no longer being required after June 1949. This was probably helped by the fact that it received renovation work at Marshalls of Cambridge after this picture was taken. (V.C.Jones)

Then the photographer has taken the rear view as the bus turns off the Embankment into Bridge Street. The passengers seem to be in a great hurry to alight. Four months after this date the vehicle was no more, having been reduced to scrap. (V.C.Jones)

Only days before eventual withdrawal from service during April 1948, STL8 works as duty X3 on Route 28 and waits before returning to Golders Green from its resting place at Wandsworth. Petrol engined with a crash gearbox, one suspects that the staff of Middle Row garage did not mind this LGOC bodied 60 seat vehicle passing into oblivion, even if it was only fifteen years of age. Turnham Green and Middle Row garages had a preponderance of these first examples of the STL class with their bodies owing much in their design to the 'Bluebird' LTs. (John McMillen)

The next vehicle waiting to depart for Dorking by way of Green Line route 713 is T437 with duty plates DS35. This Weymann bodied AEC Regal which was normally in service on Country Area bus routes in and around its Surrey home has been pressed into use on this much more arduous and prestige duty and even manages to carry a side route board on the brackets which are still in place from its pre-war use on this type of service. Disposed of to the South Wales dealer who traded as G.H.Morgan in January 1953 it was the only 9T9 to pass through their hands. Nothing is documented as to its later fate. (John McMillen)

RT647 entered service in September 1948 being the last one of the batch RT639 to RT647 put into service operating out of Grays garage. At the time it was fitted with Weymann body number 1896. In February 1964 it was disposed of to the Cape Electric Tramways in South Africa but was by then fitted with Park Royal body 2263. It had received three overhauls during the fifteen and a half years spent in the ownership of the Executive and had been operated by four Country Area garages, in sequence Grays, Tring, Garston and Windsor. Pictured on 25th September it turns out of Hogg Lane from the garage ready for a trip to Romford on 370, the route for which the batch were allocated. (V.C.Jones)

In low winter sunshine Turnham Green's ST346 is seen at Hook on Route 65. In the 1950 supplement to the 1946 book of this series the vehicle can be seen in the ownership of the Ballet Montmartre at Doncaster but here it is in its last year of London Transport duty. Having first entered service in October 1930 it was converted to operate on gas fuel between September 1943 and October 1944. It was in September 1948 at the time it was carrying body number 10669 and identified as a 1ST1/1 that it was withdrawn from the streets of London. (John McMillen)

The Green Line livery of STL2523 contrasts sharply with the Central Area red colour scheme of ST286 while both are employed on the special 406F service on 5th June 1948. In turn they will leave Epsom Station when appropriate passenger loading allows for the short journey up to the famous racecourse. The STL had reached Romford, London Road garage on 29th August 1946 together with four other STLs, one of which is shown within this supplement, to augment the fleet of utility Daimlers engaged on Green Line duties. The chassis of this bus would later be used to produce SRT56 which continued to carry registration FJJ683 in 1949. Interesting to reflect that under present licensing regulations, the SRT might well have been required to carry 'Q' prefix marks. The STL16 type body seen here would replace the Park Royal example previously fitted to STL2055 in the same period that the new SRT was being produced. (A.B.Cross)

What a sorry state of affairs greeted photographers of the era who visited the Bull Yard, Peckham, site of the later Rye Lane garage. Here on 29th February 1948 a fairly large number of discarded vehicles await their fate, the only one of which that can be positively identified being the centrally positioned LT5/1 bodied LT341. Withdrawn in July 1947 this bus hung around until April of the following year before being reduced to scrap. (John McMillen)

Rather incredibly LT1064 carries nearly a full set of glass window valances on its offside. To get through around eighteen years of public service in London including the war years and to have the first saloon window replaced in two sections and yet still retain the glass valances takes some beating. Borrowed from Edgware garage and pressed into use on Route 16 carrying W31 duty plates with route blinds already set for its return journey to Cricklewood, the bus is replacing an ST or STL which were the normal fare on this road. Also visible in the picture is Leyton garaged LT261 in use on Route 38, an unidentifiable ST to follow the single deck LT on Route 16 while Victoria based STL2178 will soon be departing for Mill Hill on Route 52. (John Gascoine collection)

A trio of Camberwell's mechanics have decided to attend to the problems of a couple of STLs in the fine sunshine prevailing on Saturday 24th April 1948. STL454, a 2/16STL18 variant and sister STL2369 of 4/9STL14/1 configuration now have their front axles sitting on wooden blocks to have their brake shoe and lining assemblies replaced, examples of which can be seen lying around. This particular view brings back happy memories to the author who remembers carrying out similar duties in the yard of Chelverton Road, Putney garage on RT type family buses. (V.C.Jones)

Normally resident at Addlestone garage, STL1488, which has only recently lost its 'b' suffix, now sits within the Dorking garage yard on 6th March 1948 complete with DS30 running plates. Makeshift route details are displayed for its use on Green Line 712 relief duties and of interest is the carefully made 'Green Line' slipboard which has been slotted in place by the platform. Finishing service with London Transport while garaged at St.Albans in June 1951 this front entrance Weymann bodied bus was disposed of the following month. Later the body was converted to open top while in the ownership of the University of London Institute of Education. (John McMillen)

On 11th September 1948 red liveried ST512, on loan from Upton Park garage, works on Route 371 from its temporary home of Grays showing Purfleet, Tunnel Garage as its next destination. Having been used in the provinces from August 1942 through to the same month two years later the bus was quickly returned to work in the Central Area but here yet again it has found itself on unfamiliar roads. (A.B.Cross)

Compare this view of ST1138 at West Croydon carrying a standard ST1/1 body to that which appeared on page 122 of the 1939-45 book of this series when its original ST9 'provincial' style body was still in evidence. It was in March 1942 that the exchange took place and the bus was transformed into just another ordinary looking ST. Only its Hertfordshire registration suggested that further investigation might be needed. Reigate garage housed this bus for many years and even after withdrawal from public service in July 1949 continued using it in a learner capacity until early the following year when it was dispatched for its inevitable fate at the hands of Daniels' workforce.

Although repainted into red livery upon receiving an overhaul in June 1948, STL1922 was continuing to operate from Watford High Street garage when seen on 23rd July. It waits to take up duties on Route 311 looking extremely smart. In January 1945 it had gained green livery having first entered service in May 1937 in Central Area red colours. With the first arrivals of post-war RTs at WA in September the bus moved down to Kingston which was a much more appropriate garage for its current colour scheme. This 4/9STL14 last saw service from Sutton being withdrawn in April 1954 and was later employed by Beeline Roadways Ltd. of West Hartlepool. (V.C.Jones)

At least three forms of transport are depicted in this view at the junction of City Road and Goswell Road approaching the Angel, Islington. The main subject is LT1042, a stalwart of Muswell Hill garage which on 2nd December 1948 finds itself using unfamiliar roads as it is pressed into service on Route 43 between London Bridge and Friern Barnet. This route usually employed double deck variants of the same class while Routes 210, 212, 244 and 251 serving the northern suburbs around Muswell Hill were the normal home of this single decker. Note the poor condition of the road surface and the railway company employee in charge of his horse and dray who looks a little fed up with his lot. (A.B.Cross)

Gleaming Park Royal bodied RT218 from Potters Bar garage is seen at Victoria Station surrounded by an assortment of other types of buses some of which have only a very short lifespan with London Transport to complete. On the left another Park Royal product is mounted on a Guy Arab I chassis to form G3 housed at Tottenham garage and soon to depart for Stoke Newington by way of Route 76. An LT on Route 29 can be seen behind the new RT while the RT on the right of the picture working Route 38A carries the first type of offside route number plate added to the new vehicles. Another LT on Route 38 completes the picture. (L.T.P.S.)

In the late summer of 1948 Hammersmith garaged ST172 is seen making its way to Chessington Zoo at the Fountain public house, New Malden. A van version of the Ford Popular Series Y is parked beside the kerb in a spot which would probably attract the swift attention of traffic wardens today. Sadly before the end of the year this bus with its Strachan built body number 11476, one of only fifty from this manufacturer for the ST class, was destined to become only a memory, meeting its final demise at the hands of the breakers. (A.B.Cross)

The first batch of standard Green Line coaches consisting of T51 to T149, T155 and T157 to T207 were of petrol engined AEC Regal chassis with rear entrance bodies built variously by the LGOC, Hall Lewis & Co.Ltd. or Short Bros. Delivery commenced in April 1930 and was completed by October, the classification 7T7 being allocated to the entire batch. With the arrival of the 10T10 LPTB bodied variety all were withdrawn as coaches during 1938. Although disposal of them began in May 1938, it was a long drawn out affair. Some were retained and reappeared in use as buses, others were converted for use in the service fleet while a small number even found themselves back on Green Line duties, including T66 shown here. This vehicle was eventually sold to the War Department for Control Commission, Germany in May 1945 and shipped to the continent. It is seen here after sale to the civilian market with rebuilt offside entrance door to its original body and carries French registration 4270MD9 on 4th October 1948 in use on the Jules Lescomptre service which operated between Douai and Esquerchin. (J.H.Price)

ST842 waits at Kingston Station ready for a short working to Epsom on Route 406. This petrol engined bus was first registered for service in June 1930 to operate from Bromley garage with Thomas Tilling Ltd. and it soldiered on until September 1948. A temporary exile to Walsall Corporation for a period which lasted a little over two years during the war it spent the major part of 1947 and 1948 allocated to the Country Area at Leatherhead as seen here. (John McMillen)

Tring garage was the first recipient of the Country Area liveried post war 3RT3 buses and very handsome they looked too. RT598 is pictured on one of its earliest outings in July 1948 being the second RT to wear the Lincoln green. It is making its way to Aylesbury from Watford Junction and having just passed Two Waters garage it still has a fair part of the route to cover before reaching its destination. The Weymann built body carries London Transport number 1847. Note the radiator badge which in keeping with the main body colour has been changed from the blue variety worn by the Central Area vehicles to pale green. (L.Housden collection)

With a background, which today is completely unrecognisable apart from the top of Kingston Station just visible above the hoardings, T40 has arrived from Weybridge on Route 219. Having set down its passengers in Cromwell Road it will turn right into the rear of Kingston bus garage before passing through to the bus station facing on to Clarence Street. It was January 1930 that T40 entered public service being garaged at the time at Holloway for use on Route 110, now the 210. 44 of the 49 T class buses which entered service between December 1929 and January 1930 with rear entrances were rebuilt to front entrance configuration in line with the fiftieth bus of the order, T156, which had that arrangement from new. This latter vehicle was the first front entrance bus of any kind in the LGOC fleet. The remaining five buses, T15,21,25,26 and 35, were all disposed of still in original condition having spent their time in the Country Area of operations. T40 was to receive a further rebuild by Marshall's of Cambridge in April 1949 which ensured it would continue in LT ownership until July 1953. (John McMillen)

Journeying through Croydon on its way to Croydon Airport, Elmers End garaged LT502 is hotly pursued by an STL bus and tramcar in traffic free conditions. An exchange from petrol to diesel propulsion was carried out in November 1933 and attention given to the bodywork by Mann Egerton in June 1946 which helped in no small way to the LTs longevity, it being withdrawn from service as late as October 1949. After that it passed into the hands of R.L.Daniels and was duly scrapped along with so many of its contemporaries. (W.J.Haynes)

This rear view of ST914 working the short 42 route from Aldgate to Camberwell Green shows the rounded features of these vehicles which, although antiquated, were nevertheless aesthetically pleasing. The fittings beneath the roller blind box once held the via points board, the use of which appears to have fallen out of favour during World War II. This view was captured on film on 21st August 1948 at a moment when only a couple of trolleybuses could be seen in an otherwise quiet Trolleybus and Green Line Coach Station at Aldgate. (V.C.Jones)

ST722 of 1931 vintage is now beginning to look a little tired in this view taken at Camberwell garage in April 1948 having just passed its eighteenth birthday. It appears to be receiving some sort of mechanical attention with two fitters in the lower saloon and a toolbox perched on the platform. At the top of the rearmost window to the lower saloon a Route 40 stencil is slotted into the brackets which were added in wartime while a pre-war style route blind adorns the route box. One of the large number of this type of vehicle then housed at Camberwell, it still had three more official garage transfers to complete before finally being withdrawn from service in January 1950. (V.C.Jones)

A comparison between the front end styling of two different body builders' products is afforded by this print of ST884 and ST1094 resting from their respective duties. The bus nearest the camera, originally owned by Thomas Tilling Ltd., carries either a Dodson or a Tilling built body, the two manufacturers' products on this batch of vehicles being indistinguishable. The Tilling style indicator boxes on these vehicles were always a problem in later years. In this case it seems a blind has been cut down to fit, resulting in the odd destination 'BERKHAMST'. The slightly more modern looking ST1094, originally owned by the East Surrey Traction Company, is fitted with a Ransomes, Sims and Jefferies fully enclosed body and actually entered service four months earlier than the open staircase example. (D.W.K.Jones)

LT1081 seen in service from Muswell Hill garage on Route 251 and parked on the stand outside Arnos Grove Station ready for another run through the rural surroundings of Totteridge to Burnt Oak, Edgware Road. This same vehicle appears in the 1950 supplement to the 1946 book of this series after it was converted to a lorry. It was in September 1949 that it finished its service career while still garaged at Muswell Hill to pass through the hands of the Rainham dealer, R.Daniels. (A.B.Cross)

Languishing on the bomb site situated at York Road, Waterloo, later to become the site of the Festival of Britain, ex-London Transport service vehicle 16S, formerly open top bus S384, still awaits a purchaser. For the princely sum of £20 someone could have bought themselves this piece of history last used by the LPTB as a tree lopper. At present it is unknown whether anyone took up the offer or if the vehicle was eventually reduced to scrap but what a great pity the preservation movement had not got under way in 1948. (Norman Anscomb collection)

This interior view is looking forward in the lower saloon of the lowbridge Short Bros. body carried by ST136. Quite clearly one can observe the sunken gangways of the upper saloon protruding into the lower deck and the 'caution low roof' notices fixed to the seat backs. AEC, the chassis maker's initials, adorn the clutch housing at the front of the saloon while bare bulbs provide the illumination. The curtain at the front is provided for the driver's benefit to stop any saloon glare distracting his attention and would be drawn by the conductor in the hours of darkness. Note that no stanchions are provided although stepped grab handles are in evidence on the seat backs. This picture should remind a few travellers of the times they have bumped their heads when rising from their seats! (V.C.Jones)

RT183 now carries its legal owner's new title in the form of a temporary sticker while seen loading passengers at the Royal Forest Hotel, Chingford for a journey to Victoria by way of Route 38. The fact that passengers are boarding from a queue opposite the bus stand indicates this is either a Summer Sunday or a Bank Holiday. At least two Gs, an STL and two LTs occupy the stand outside the hotel with Queen Elizabeth's Hunting Lodge to the far right. The damaged front dome to Park Royal body number 1432 spoils an otherwise nicely turned out vehicle and incidently when disposed of in November 1958 this body was still matched to its original chassis. (S.L.Poole)

APPENDIX I

London Transport Central and Country Area Bus Garages

Code	Garage	Code	Garage
A	Sutton	HN*	Hitchin
AB	Twickenham	HW	Hanwell
AC	Willesden	J	Holloway
AD	Palmers Green	K	Kingston
AE	Hendon	L	Loughton
AF	Chelverton Road, Putney	LH*	Leatherhead
AH	Nunhead	LS*	Luton
AK	Streatham	M	Mortlake
AL	Merton	MA*	Amersham
AM	Plumstead	MH	Muswell Hill
AP	Seven Kings	N	Norwood
AR	Tottenham	NF*	Northfleet
AV	Hounslow	ON	Alperton
B	Battersea	P	Old Kent Road
BK	Barking	PB	Potters Bar
C	Athol Street, Poplar	Q	Camberwell
CF	Chalk Farm	R	Hammermsith
CL	Clay Hall	RD	Hornchurch
CM*	Chelsham	RE*	London Road, Romford
CS	Chiswick (non-operational)	RG*	Reigate
CY*	Crawley	S	Shepherds Bush
D	Dalston	SA*	St.Albans
DG*	Dunton Green	SJ*	Swanley Junction
DS*	Dorking	SP	Sidcup
DT*	Dartford	ST*	Staines
E	Enfield	T	Leyton
ED	Elmers End	TB	Bromley
EG*	East Grinstead	TC	Croydon
EP*	Epping	TG*	Tring
EW	Edgware	TL	Catford
F	Putney Bridge	TW*	Tunbridge Wells
G	Forest Gate	U	Upton Park
GD*	Godstone	UX	Uxbridge
GF*	Guildford	V	Turnham Green
GM	Gillingham Street, Victoria	W	Cricklewood
GY*	Grays	WA*	Watford High Street
H	Hackney	WG	West Green
HD	Harrow Weald	WR*	Windsor
HE*	High Wycombe	WT*	Leavesden Road, Watford
HF*	Hatfield	WY*	Addlestone
HG*	Hertford	X	Middle Row
HH*	Two Waters, Hemel Hempstead		

* indicates a Country Area garage.

The above list is of all operational motorbus garages available in 1947. There were no changes from the previous year.

APPENDIX II

Again a special thank you is extended to the following correspondents for their interest shown in updating or correcting information given in earlier titles in this series of books and in some cases answering queries arising in preparation of the present volume. They are: Laurie Akehurst, Eric S.Baker, Tony Beard of the '2RT2 Preservation Society', Christopher G.Edwards, Dr.K.M.Gregory, Mike Jordan, Graham Lockyer, Barry Maynard-Smith, John McMillen, Lewis Norris, Graham Smith, James Stirling of 'Allsorts', Michael R.B.Taylor, Bob Williamson, Frank Willis and Alan Wood.

1939 - 1945 BOOK

Page 74 ST237 is pictured at Huntingdon Street Bus Station, Nottingham rather than Grantham as originally stated.

Page 75 Route 254 became double deck operated and renumbered on 1st September 1940, not two months on from when the picture was taken in 1939 as stated in the caption.

Page 101 A copy of an official document has now been received which confirms that RT97 was not repaired by Birmingham City Transport to whom it was dispatched soon after receiving enemy inflicted damage in 1944. Further research is now no longer required as mentioned in Appendix II of the 1946 book.

Page 150 The car with the gas bag mounted on the roof is a late version Series III Morris 14.

1946 BOOK

Page 60 Of interest is the fact that the bus shelter shown in the lower picture is made of steel. The second generation of this type of structure which began to appear in the 1950s were manufactured from aluminium.

Page 65 The air raid shelters seen in the background are those that once stood on the triangular site adjoining Bush Road, Leytonstone.

Page 78 The blind display for Route 66 with the via points Ilford, Romford is the one intended for use on garage workings from Forest Gate garage via the 86A route to Romford and line of route. The correct display had Newbury Park, Romford via points. The other garage working was via Woodgrange Rd. as shown by C88 on page 92.

Page 82 My apologies to all concerned! The particular body carried by STL1199 is of classification STL11, being one of the first fifty of the type built. These first examples of the large number manufactured kept the STL5 front blind box arrangement together with sidelights in the STL11 position.

Page 83 ST141 is pictured standing at the Leavesden Road terminus in Watford.

Page 92 When Route 62 was introduced on 4th January 1922 it first employed single deck B class vehicles rather than the K type and they were housed at Kingston garage.

Page 94 Prior to being named 'McGinty's Irish Pub' the premises in the background of the lower picture were named 'The Iron Bridge Tavern' and frequented by many AEC employees.

Page 108 T515c still wears its medium and light green livery which also adorned a number of ex-Green Line EMS ambulances during the war. It was damaged at Elmers End garage on 18th July 1944.

Page 109 Note that STD103 in the lower picture still had a grey roof when photographed in August 1942.

Page 112 It has been pointed out that this picture is a useful reminder that a full set of blinds could still be seen lingering on into 1942.

Page 114 Close inspection of the upper photograph of ST962 shows the ramp which was carried for the benefit of wheelchair users.

Page 118 G169 passes the Odeon Cinema which once stood adjacent to the 'Toby Jug' at the junction of the A3 and A240 at Tolworth, not Shannon Corner as stated. This building was much older and smaller than the 'super' cinema styled example which was incorrectly quoted in the original caption.

Page 137 The location of the bottom picture is the Custom House Station terminus of this special service.

Page 138 In the lower picture C30 is viewed standing in Parkstone Avenue near its junction with Wingletye Lane, Emerson Park.

Page 149 The caption should have stated that 733J is in company with two other service vehicles, namely a Beford tipper truck being parked further along the road and a Morris tilt-van which is on the other side of the road opposite the tower wagon.

1948 BOOK

Page 35 In the lower picture a Series E Morris '8' two door saloon is parked behind ST850.

1949 BOOK

Page 51 A rare Morris '25' carrying a March 1934 Surrey registration stands behind the STL.

Page 125 a '£100' Ford 8 h.p. car is parked behind STL2657.

1950 BOOK

Page 142 The top picture of TD50 is taken at 'The Bear' in Noak Hill Road.

1951 BOOK

Page 87 The leading of the two cars seen in the distance is a 1929/30 Rover 10 h.p. coupe with central bar 'mod' applied to the flat radiator.

Page 89 A 1932 Standard 'Big Nine' 9/10 h.p. car comes into view behind STL1055.

1955 BOOK

Page 17 The bottom picture of RTW38 shows it at the St.Pauls Road stand in Barking.

Page 70 The Royal Albert Dock terminus in use by buses since 1936 and referred to in the upper photograph was moved in the later 1970s to the junction of East Ham Manor Way and Cyprus Place the display becoming Cyprus - Royal Albert Dock. With the opening of the DLR the display was again changed and is now referred to as Cyprus Station.